Racquet Sports
An Illustrated Guide
by Elinor Nickerson

McFarland & Company, Inc., Publishers
Jefferson, N.C. & London

Library of Congress Cataloging in Publication Data

Nickerson, Elinor B.
  Racquet Sports.

  Bibliography: p.
  Includes index.
  1. Racket games. I. Title.
GV990.N53 1982   796.34   82-17180

ISBN 0-89950-051-X

Manufactured in the United States of America

for my husband
Richard A. Nickerson

Acknowledgments

Special Thanks

C.C. Pell, Racquet and Tennis Club, New York; Manhattan Tennis Club, New York; Alameda Sporting Goods, Alameda, California; Tennis Town, Pleasanton, California; United States Court Tennis Association; North American Racquets Association; United States Paddle Tennis Association; National Paddleball Association; American Platform Tennis Association; United States Squash Racquets Association; The American Badminton Association; The United States Racquetball Association; Candace Lyle Hogan, freelance; and Richard A. Nickerson, husband.

Credits

Photography

Clifford L. Gertz, Alamo, California (tennis, platform tennis, racquetball, badminton, handball, playground racquet sports).

Bill Dickinson, *Boston Phoenix* (court tennis, racquets, squash racquets).

Cary Herz, *New York Times* (table tennis).

Chapter 1. Court Tennis

Berry Toates, professional singles champion, 1976; club professional, Racquet and Tennis Club, Boston.

Chapter 2. Tennis

Kevin Merrick, Pacific Coast champion, mixed doubles, former varsity tennis coach, University of California, Berkeley; club professional, Orinda Country Club, Orinda, California.

Chapter 3. Platform Tennis

Kerry P. Schaeffner, Platform Tennis Incorporated, San Francisco.

Chapter 4. Table Tennis

Marty Reisman, United States and world championship holder, Reisman's Table Tennis, New York.

Chapter 5. Racquets

Berry Toates, club professional, Racquet and Tennis Club, Boston.

Chapter 6. Squash Racquets

Darwin P. Kingsley III, president, United States Squash Racquets Association, Bala Cynwyd, Pennsylvania.

Chapter 7. Racquetball

Rob Hammer, club professional, Supreme Court II, San Carlos, California.

Chapter 8. Badminton

Jerry Eichelberger, Executive Council member, American Badminton Association, United States Thomas Team captain, 1974, Hayward, California.

Research Consultant, sports history

Dr. Alyce T. Cheska, The Association for the Anthropological Study of Play, University of Illinois, Urbana/Champaign, Illinois.

Graphics

J and D Graphics, Walnut Creek, California.

Facilities and Models

Racquet and Tennis Club, Boston (court tennis, racquets, squash racquets).
Supreme Court II, San Carlos, California (racquetball).
Reisman's Table Tennis, New York (table tennis).
The Merrick Residence, Alamo, California (tennis).
College of Notre Dame, Belmont, California (platform tennis).
Wilbur Junior High School, Palo Alto, California (badminton).
The Racquetball Club, Walnut Creek (handball, playground racquet games).

Judy Balco, Sarah Barrows, Rodney Barton, Kim Bishop, Dennis Bourke, Deborah Brickley, James Cannon, Margaret Cockerton, Bell Colucci, Drew Colucci, Jodie Colucci, Barbara Cotrell, Frank Costello, Vi Croop, Greg Ditchley, Jerry Eichelberger, Martha Fefley, Peter Forbes, Joyce Fulton, Wendy Garrels, Alice Green, Robert Hamm, Gerry Ippolito, Judy Kaine, Marc Kennedy, Margo Kennedy, Robert Kraut, Beth Larsen, Del Larsen, Benny Lee, Chuck Libby, Joe McDonald, Pat McKenna, John McKenna, Donna McNulty, Kathy McNulty, Kerry McNulty, Judy Merrick, Kelly Merrick, Kevin Merrick, Shannon Merrick, Harold Morris, Dick Ng, Lea Neu, Jim Olson, Steven Peck, Carolyn Penn, Jennifer Powell, Kenneth Roper, Stephen Ryan, Glenn Sahara, Kerry Schaeffner, Mark Sedgwick, Fred Spencer, Roger Sverdlik, Barry Toates, Don Tringale, Joseph White, Frederic Work, David Yonemoto.

Contents

Foreword

Racquet Sports: An Illustrated Guide is written about eight racquet games that people play: court tennis, (modern) tennis, platform tennis, table tennis, racquets, squash (actually squash racquets), racquetball, and badminton. A ninth game, handball, is included, for it uses the original racquet of all, the palm of the hand. (The present nearly symbiotic relationship between racquetball and handball has helped the growth of both games. Played on identical courts, both sports patronize the same facilities and help keep the expensive new racquetball complexes solvent.) Most of these games are played by both men and women, adults and children. Some are played almost exclusively by relatively young men, one by men of means and position, one by almost nobody. All can be played and enjoyed in some form so long as a player can grasp a racquet (or extend a hand) and move around. Most grant instant success, meaning instant fun, within minutes of a player's introduction to the game. Others require months of work before enough skill can be learned for one to be able to say, "I am a player." And in none of these sports can any player truly claim to have learned everything there is to learn.

In doing the research for this book the author was repeatedly caught up by the anthropological premise that all racquet sports can be traced to a common ancestor. In the earliest records of play, pictures of men, women and children found in the most ancient of archeological digs show them striking a round object with the hand. Later the hand wears a glove. Still later the glove is replaced by another object (i.e., a racquet), thereby creating an extension of power and changing the dynamics of the game.

Hictorically it is known that *jeu de paume* evolved to court tennis, a sport which once shook up kingdoms. Now we have table tennis, paddle tennis, platform tennis and lawn tennis, a game with its own royalty. Handball evolved into racquets, squash, paddleball, and the modern craze for racquetball, a sport now doing some kingdom-shaking of its own.

Some tantalizing questions remain unanswered. For example, why are there differences in spelling. *Racquets* is preferred in North America and *rackets* in Great Britain. Why do some games award points only to the serving team, others to either server or receiver? What accounts for the unusual point names and point system in the tennis games?

This book is written for the current player and also for the would-be player or follower of racquet sports. The author has emphasized the commonalities and the differences among the sports, isolating them for purposes of analysis, then blending them into the overall presentation of game skills and strategy. Most people will find that the many differences are not so great after all and that some of the commonalities emerge as interesting differences in reality. The book is based on the principle that if you play and like one racquet sport you can find other racquet games you will enjoy equally well. The skills of one sport carry over into others. So does the zest. Only in the case of the dedicated professional in one particular sport might a case be made that play of another sport adversely affects play in the one. For the rest of us, quite the reverse will be true.

Each chapter considers history, the nature of the game, equipment, clothing, play of the ball, fundamental movements, courtesies, rules, professional play, and organizations. Each chapter is fully illustrated.

A last chapter deals with playground racquet sports, those less formal games which can lead up to the more competitive sports.

Comments from the sidelines, an annotated bibliography of further reading, and a detailed index complete the book.

Chapter 1

Court Tennis

History

Court tennis, as it is often called in the United States (it is known as *real tennis* in England, *royal tennis* in Australia, and *jeu de paume* in France), is the ancestor, direct or indirect, of all racquet sports played today. The historical trail of this antique game is clear and strong as far back as the 12th century. Then the trail dims, becoming obscured for lack of written records.

The words "tennis" and "racquets," so confidently used in the names of many modern sports, also have origins lost in time. Does "tennis" come from the French, *tenez* (originally *tenetz*), which meant "take heed" or "play"? Or does the word come from an ancient Egyptian city on the Nile called "Tanis" by the Greeks and "Tinnis" by the Arabs? Is "racquet" derived from the Arabic word *rahat*, meaning "palm of the hand"? The word "hazard," used to designate one end of the tennis court, also invites speculation. In Arabic it meant "dice," later "chance." Does this, too, imply a Mideast origin for the court tennis game?

Anthropological studies show that early Christian clergy were devoted to a tennis-like game (still played by hand) which formed a part of an annual Easter festival up until the 13th century. The game of *la soule* appears to be "none other than the origin of tennis, and all those amusements in which one strikes or struggles for a ball," according to Robert W. Henderson (in *Ball, Bat and Bishop,* Rockport Press, New York, 1947), citing the 1859 scholar, A.D. Barthelemey. Prior to the 10th century, ball games leave a spotty trail back long

1

before Christian times, with polo emerging as the most ancient of games played with stick and ball. The Tibetan word, *pulu,* meaning ball, is the antecedent for *polo*; one might thus speculate even that this ball game had a Tibetan or Chinese origin. Authorities agree that the Persian game spread eastward as far as Japan and have established that all of these games were played in conjunction with religious occasions, particularly ancient springtime rites.

In A.D. 1170, in Byzantium (Istanbul), ball games involving sticks for striking implements were still played on horseback, but another form of the game, *la soule,* had been developed in which a large ball was played between two teams on foot. These games, it is believed, had also evolved from the ancient fertility rites brought by the Moors from Northern Africa, across the Mediterranean, through Spain to southern and western France. Henderson also refers to Lady Wentworth's suggestion that the Persians had two sorts of ball games: "one called *salvajan,* played with a stick curved or hooked at the end, which was obviously the origin of polo. The other, *chigan,* sometimes spelled *Tchaugan,* was played with a *shorter and stringed racket* [italics added] and must have been the origin of the French *chicane*, or jeu de paume [tennis] and the Greek game, *Tzanisterium.*"

As Christianity gained power in Europe, the old customs were Christianized. Henderson is careful to state that the Moors brought Islamic rites, rather than the games of ball, tennis, and polo, and that these rites were modified by customs of different localities in keeping with local religious persuasions of the time. In the 12th century, *la soule* appears to have added a stringed bat to the game (the ball could now be driven by foot, bat, or hand), and nobility and ecclesiastics enjoyed the game enthusiastically during Shrovetide. Reference is made to *chouler à la crosse* in a letter dated 1381, thus apparently identifying the origin of lacrosse.

It can be seen that anthropologists have developed quite a brief for a common origin of ball games, with little trouble accounting for the link-up with polo, soccer, and lacrosse. To make a reasonable connection between striking a ball with a sturdy mallet on the ground of a large field while astride a galloping horse and hitting a ball by hand or racquet over a net in a relatively small enclosure requires a considerable amount of faith. Nevertheless the clear link between earliest ball games and tennis is believed to exist, only awaiting discovery. For instance, many modern scholars believe that the game of *pila* or *pilota,* the antecedent for *jai alai* and mentioned in the "Rules of the Religious Chapter of Auxere in 1396 as Played in Accordance with Easter Festivities," has demonstrable kinship with *la soule.*

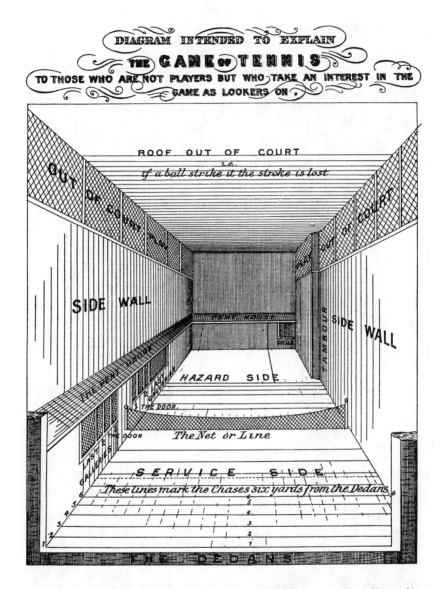

DIAGRAM INTENDED TO EXPLAIN
THE GAME OF TENNIS
TO THOSE WHO ARE NOT PLAYERS BUT WHO TAKE AN INTEREST IN THE
GAME AS LOOKERS ON.

ROOF OUT OF COURT
i.e.
if a ball strike it the stroke is lost

OUT OF COURT

OUT OF COURT

SIDE WALL

SIDE WALL

TAMBOUR

THE NET POST

THE LAST GALLERIES

HAZARD SIDE

THE DOOR.

THE DOOR

LAST GALLERIES

The Net or Line

S E R V I C E   S I D E

These lines mark the Chases six yards from the Dedans

THE DEDANS

In any case, whatever its origin, historical records affirm that
court tennis was extremely popular in France from the 12th century
onward. First played in open court and stable yards of Christian
churches and monasteries, using only the hand to strike the ball, it
took three more centuries before aching fingers and swollen palms
were replaced by stringed racquets. Year by year the religious
significance of the game dwindled until, at last, court tennis emerged

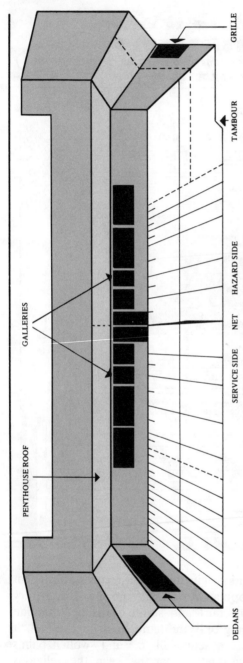

PENTHOUSE ROOF

GALLERIES

GRILLE

TAMBOUR

DEDANS

SERVICE SIDE   NET   HAZARD SIDE

The penthouse is covered with a wooden, slanting roof, and slopes down at 45 degrees from the wall. It extends along the endwall behind the server, all along the sidewall to his left, and along the endwall behind the receiver.

The wall to the server's right, known as the main wall, has no penthouse.

The dedans is the large rectangular opening in the wall at the server's end of the court. The choice seats are located here behind a heavy net protecting the spectators.

The grille is a small opening, 3 feet, 1 inch square, in the wall at the opposite end of the court.

The tambour is a projection of the main wall—the side on the right as viewed by the server, the wall without a penthouse. The projection is in the receiver's or hazard end of the court, starting about 6 feet from the end of the court, slanting 18 inches into the court at a 45 degree angle, and continuing in a straight line to the hazard endwall. A ball striking this buttress, from the server's end ricochets

at varying angles, often catching the player at the hazard end flatfooted.

There is a series of compartments in the side penthouse wall, extending 24 feet from the net on each side. These openings, separated by iron posts, are known, from the net, as first gallery, door, second gallery, and last gallery. The last gallery on the side on which the grille and tambour are found—the hazard side—is called the winning gallery.

as a completely secularized game. Replications of the original court-yards appeared. Casual rules stabilized as formal "laws" of play. The game evolved into another of those known as "the sport of kings."

The earliest attempt to define and codify rules is found in a lengthy treatise compiled by the Italian abbot, Antonio Scaino, in 1555. Later rules were written by a Frenchman, Forget, in 1592, and printed by Haulpean in 1599 and 1632. The game, once played almost exclusively out-of-doors, in whatever court or enclosure came to hand, moved indoors. Sumptuous arenas were built by wealthy nobility, the most noteworthy being Hampton Court Palace in England (still in use), the court at Versailles, and the court near the Louvre (now an art gallery called the Jeu de Paume). It is reported that in the year 1600, Paris alone had 1,800 tennis courts, along with a like number of professional tennis masters.

Court tennis reached its peak in England and France during the 16th and 17th centuries. By this time the players were almost exclusively men of power, station, and nobility while the general public took part in much gambling on the contests. Inevitably scandal and crookedness infested the gaming, and the sport began its long decline into relative obscurity. The French Revolution, the civil strife in England, and the changing life styles of the world in the late 19th and early 20th centuries all hastened its fall from popularity. From the thousands of courts once teeming with players, there now remain only a few exclusive clubs and a handful of members who play the game.

Just how and when court tennis came to the United States is not exactly known. Reference is made in a document credited to Peter Stuyvesant, governor of New York, dated September 30, 1659, in relation to a "service of thanksgiving ... to interdict and forbid during divine service ... all exercise and games of tennis." Ships arriving at the colony of New Amsterdam in the early 1700s advertised among their cargo racquets and balls, presumably having a market for this equipment. But no amount of research has ever turned up the location of a tennis court at that time.

The first record of court construction in the United States is in Boston in 1876. Later a few other courts were built on the East Coast. But court tennis never really had a chance in the United States. At the time of the Boston court's construction, lawn tennis, an offspring of court tennis, had already found its way to Long Island in the vacation luggage of Miss Mary Outerbridge. (In February, 1874: see the chapter on lawn tennis.) Soon this upstart would overwhelm and almost totally replace the parent game.

Now the United States has but seven court tennis facilities still

in use: two in New York City, and one each in Tuxedo, N.Y., Boston, Aiken, S.C., Philadelphia, and Manhasset, N.Y. England's courts are limited to 17, France has two, Australia has three, and Scotland, two.

These few playing areas represent the last bastions of people who can best be described as votaries of the game. Their love of the game is unquestionable, but the pitifully small cadre of players, estimated as a mere 300 in the United States, may well leave too limited a pool of talent to support the game in spite of recurring attempts to recruit new players. Publicity for court tennis is welcomed in some centers, yet a wariness of exploitation often overpowers the desire to spread the word. The only glimpse most people can hope to have of court tennis in action is from a three minute fragment of film in the 1976 movie, *The Seven Percent Solution,* in which two players elect to fight a duel by playing tennis on a "real" tennis court. It is a hyped-up sequence, both in sound and action, and hardly resembles an actual contest.

Indeed, "real tennis" is the name most players still use in referring to their favorite sport. Whether or not the game will survive much longer is open to speculation, but meanwhile, among an exclusive few, the game continues even though it may not be flourishing.

The Game

Court tennis, when viewed for the first time, appears to be a sedate, leisurely sport requiring rather modest skills executed with a degree of finesse: an antique game which demands little sustained effort — a totally misleading impression. Played indoors by two players (singles) or two players on a side (doubles), the game superficially resembles lawn tennis. A ball is struck back and forth across a net by contestants wielding stringed racquets. Points carry names like "fifteen," "thirty," "forty," "deuce," and "advantage," all nomenclature familiar to the modern sports world. But unlike the sharp, crisp beat heard in lawn tennis when the racquet meets the ball, the sound of a court tennis hit is muted, slightly softened, which also contributes to the low-keyed impression. The sight of the playing arena adds further to the illusion of stateliness and antiquity. In fact, the first visit to a court tennis match is like a step into the past.

Opposite: The austerity of the real tennis court is reminiscent of gymnasia of half a century past. The netted "galleries" are said to represent stalls for livestock.

The game is played indoors on a replica of a medieval court-yard, including shed roof, rectangular openings into what appear to have once been livestock stalls, flying buttress, an entrance to a buttery, posts and other various doorways; all formalized and standardized throughout eight centuries of play. Heavy corded nets block off the rectangular openings called "galleries." (Indeed, "gallery" is the name given to the viewing audience of all tennis matches, lawn and court alike, and is also used to describe the spectators at other racquet sports.)

Unlike lawn tennis, where symmetry is the rule in court design and game plan, court tennis depends on asymmetry for much of its challenge. The red-tinted, concrete floor, measuring 110 by 38 feet for both doubles and singles play (as compared to 78 by 27 feet for singles lawn tennis), is bisected by a heavy, cumbersome net drooping from five feet at the walls to three feet at the middle. Running around three sides of the court is a sloping shed roof, seven feet wide, properly called the "penthouse." Far up, at least 30 feet above floor level, light filters down from a skylighted ceiling aided by turn-of-the-century lighting hanging from old-fashioned gymnasium electric fixtures. The asymmetry of the game is further exemplified in the court markings. Each side is marked differently and in accord with the rather complicated rules of the game. (See illustration.)

One half of the court surface is called the "service side" from which the serve is delivered. Lines, called "chase lines," are marked off, parallel to the net, in one yard and half-yard increments. The wall immediately behind the player in this court has an opening or gallery beneath the penthouse roof called the "dedans." Traditionally the spectators (the gallery) view the game from behind this enclosure. Opposite the service side is the receiving side, called the "hazard" side. Chase lines are marked on only half of this side, beginning at the net. Between the last chase line and the wall to the back of the hazard player (called the "hazard wall"), with the exception of a small area to the hazard player's left (marked by a line called the "pass line"), lies the legal service area or "box" to which the ball is delivered at the start of play. In the hazard wall, to the player's left, the "grille" is cut: an opening approximately three feet by three feet, the bottom level being about four feet from the floor. (Historically, the grille is said to represent the buttery, hence the belief that the side galleries were once

Opposite: Few out-of-bounds areas exist to restrict play. There are no sidelines or endlines. The ceiling and the lighter spaces above the walls are out of play.

cow sheds rather than horse stalls.) The last feature of the hazard side is the "tambour," a projection resembling a flying buttress, which intrudes about one and a half feet into the court on the "main wall" to the left of the hazard player for approximately 21 feet along the side of the wall. The end of the tambour closest to the net tapers obliquely. Balls rebounding from this angle are often winners and always difficult to play. Finally, a half court line bisects the floor from the dedans wall to the grille wall.

The four walls (the grille, the main, the dedans, and the side wall), are constructed from dark, almost black concrete. The slick concrete of the longer walls extends to a height of 18 feet, the shorter walls to 23 feet, and constitute the legal areas of play for shots rebounding from them. Entrance to the court is through two openings by the net at the side wall, beneath its penthouse.

Below the net runs a shallow gutter, for trapping tennis balls. A large wicker basket is set into a small well at the penthouse side of the net and is used for collecting balls. Wooden troughs in the galleries under the penthouses are set into the concrete away from the playing surfaces. These are for the convenience of collecting and storing tennis balls. Unlike lawn tennis, where players often supply their own tennis balls and a pair or two are used repeatedly throughout a series of games, court tennis balls belong to the tennis club. A minimum of 72 balls are put into play. (It has been said as recently as the 17th century that the trousseau of a "lady" still included six dozen tennis balls in a wicker basket, hence the traditional method for collecting and storing.) Balls which have fallen and are out of play are pushed toward the gutter. The server reaches into the dedans tray for a ball when ready to serve. When all 72 balls are in the gutter area, play is halted and balls are swept into the basket, then taken to the more convenient location in the dedans trough.

In spite of the unique surroundings and the strange vocabulary of court tennis, the newcomer need not be intimidated. Experienced players will sometimes compare the game to chess, polo, billiards, and lawn tennis in referring to court strategy and plain muscle power, and in so doing will either intentionally or unintentionally put off the would-be learner, but it is not at all difficult to grasp its fundamentals and as the intricacies emerge, the game's challenge cannot be ignored.

Probably the most revealing moments come when the new player has the first "hit" on the court, as the warmup is called. The reality of the immense court (4,180 square feet in comparison to the lawn tennis singles court of 2,106 square feet) places unanticipated physical demands on the best athlete, particularly if the player begins

Once filled, the basket of tennis balls is carried to the dedans tray and the balls are placed there for the server's convenience.

the game after a background in lawn tennis. The basic cutting strokes require a strong wrist and forearm, together with the subtle, well-controlled power of the body behind them. The deceptive ease with which experienced players move, starting and stopping as the ball rebounds from court, penthouse, or wall, cannot be learned quickly and easily. The ball seems never to be out of play until some gross error or outright winning shot ends the rally. No longer does the court tennis game appear to be stately, leisurely, the skills modest and easily learned, the finesse an affectation of no importance, the effort an easy thing to sustain. Instead it emerges as an exciting game well worth participation from the spectator's point of view, and even more exciting to play.

Equipment

The racquet

The court tennis racquet, commonly called the "tennis bat," is unique in design. The stringed portion is lop-sidedly pearshaped (see

Tennis bat and ball (left). The white ball is a finished product; beneath its cover it is tied with twine in the intricate butterfly pattern shown.

photograph). The entire bat is made of wood and is approximately 27 inches long. The best strings are heavy gut. Only the Bancroft bat is sanctioned for use in national United States Court Tennis championships. The bat is heavy, weighing close to a pound, and stiff, with none of the whippiness found in lawn tennis racquets. The handle may be grooved, or wrapped in some form of taping according to the player's preference. In spite of the USCTA ruling cited above, the 1934 rules guide states "there are no restrictions as to the shape or size of rackets."

The ball

Court tennis balls measure approximately 2½ inches in diameter and weigh about 2½ ounces. They are hand made and there are variations among balls in symmetry and response, which add another dimension to the game. Court tennis balls are traditionally the property of the courts where the game is played. They are carefully built up from tightly wound strips of cloth, soaked and molded under pressure, tied with an elaborate, traditional string webbing, then covered with a special melton cloth and stitched in the interlocking hour glass design so familiar to all tennis balls, be they court or lawn tennis. The end product is a hard ball possessing very little resiliency or bound as compared with the hollow, pressurized lawn tennis ball. As a court tennis ball loses its firmness and becomes mushy, it is removed from play and painstakingly rebuilt, often in the pro-shop of the court which owns it. The book *How to Make the Real Tennis Ball from Core to Cover*, by Richard Hamilton and Anthony Hobson (Tennis and Racquets Association, Queen's Club, London, 1977), describes explicitly the process of court tennis ball manufacture.

Clothing

Court tennis rules do not prescribe clothing. Customarily the players wear white, with little decorative coloring. Shoes are regular tennis shoes, chosen according to the player's individual preference.

Play of the Ball

The ball is put in play by the server who stands on the service side anywhere behind the chase line marking the second gallery. The ball is tossed into the air and struck so that it first touches the penthouse, then falls into the service box on the hazard side. The ball must also make contact with the penthouse on the hazard side in order to be legally delivered. The person receiving the serve, known as the "striker out," now returns the ball and play, called a "rally" or "rest," continues until some error or a winning placement or a chase is made, bringing the rally to a stop. The ball may rebound from the walls or the penthouse roof during the exchange, the chief rule being that it not touch the floor on the striker's side after being hit by the striker and that at some point it must cross over the net or around the net (as on the penthouse).

A winning placement is one in which the ball is directed properly into one of three openings: the dedans, on the service side; and the winning gallery and the grille on the hazard side. (The cow-bell hanging in the grille and the one in the winning gallery clanks when this shot is successfully executed. It is said to date from the court at Versaille when King Louis XIV was reputed to cheat. The bell removed cause for debate on this play.)

Errors are, in general, those common to other racquet sports: a ball going into the net, returned out-of-bounds, or in some way mishandled. An error results in a point for the side not committing it.

However, the outstanding difference between court tennis and

Opposite and above: The forehand, in which the racquet head moves in a decided "cut" stroke. The continental grip is used for both forehand and backhand. Note the choke on the racquet handle—a practice in keeping with modern playing styles.

other ball and racquet sports lies in the "chase" rule. Other games require that a ball be volleyed (that is, be returned before bouncing), or played after only one bounce. In court tennis, if a player allows the ball to take a second bounce, a chase has been "made" and a marker is placed at the line of the second bounce or a mental note made of it. No point is awarded, and the chase is tucked away to be "played for" later. Chases are also made when the ball is struck into any of the galleries or doors, except for the three winners previously described.

Chases form the heart of court tennis strategy, for it is only when a chase is played for that the serve changes hands and the players exchange sides. The one having batted the ball which made the chase is now the defender in the chase, the opponent being the challenger or attacker. A chase ends in one of three ways: an error, a hit to a winning

Opposite and above: The backhand, which is also a "cut" stroke.

opening, or hit in which the ball bounces twice on the defender's side. If the second bounce lands closer to the end wall beyond the chase line marking the bounce for which the chase was made, the challenger has won the chase.

Chases are played for in two situations: when two chases have been accumulated ("scored"), or when only one chase has been scored and one player is at "forty" or "advantage."

Skill in basic strokes and knowledge of rules and court strategy open up an unending variety of plays for the experienced player.

Fundamentals

Forehand

The tennis bat is held in the traditional handshake grip with the stringed face slightly open (the bat is turned a bit clockwise in the hand), a grip sometimes called the "continental" grip. Beginners choke the racquet as much as eight inches from the butt end, to give better control, whereas most advanced young players still choke up to three or four inches. Occasionally an unchoked grip is seen, but this is not in keeping with modern coaching and teaching.

The grip is the same for forehand and backhand.

The right-handed player addresses the approaching ball with the body well turned from the net, left side facing the target, feet in a closed position, knees bent, weight on the right foot. The bat is held back, wrist cocked. On execution the player steps to the left foot, knee bend is deep. On impact the wrist and arm extend, the bat cuts under the ball, the follow-through is short, the stringed face open. There is no wristiness or turn-over as the ball is met, in line with the player's left foot. The move is far more abbreviated than the long, flowing classic lawn tennis drive.

Backhand

The backhand is executed in much the same way as the forehand, but with the right side toward the net. Particular care must be taken to keep the ball well toward the net, the weight travelling forward onto the right foot at the moment of impact. The backhand is also a cut stroke, as in the forehand.

Lobs and volleys

Although lobs and volleys are legitimate in court tennis, they are seen far less often than in lawn tennis. Because the ball is not restricted to the court, both offensive and defensive plays use the walls and the penthouse for returns. Plays requiring volleys and lobs such as those seen in lawn tennis seldom occur.

The serve

Many serving styles are used in court tennis. The server may deliver the ball from any place in the area behind the second gallery, and has two tries or chances to make a good serve. The ball may be hit from either the forehand or backhand side of the strings. The server may toss the ball high, or take it almost directly out of hand. At one time the ball may be struck in a high, lazy arc to the penthouse, to bounce once before striking the service box. Another time it may race along the length of the penthouse and around the corner to the grille wall before tumbling to the court. Such traditional names as "giraffe" and "railroad" describe these serves. There is also the "poop" and the "underhand slice," serves readily imagined from their names. But, in truth, there seem to be as many serves as there are players in a club — only a small exaggeration, for at least 51 combinations of effective serves are known to exist and be regularly used.

Wall shots and penthouse shots

One of the first techniques a court tennis player learns is to pause, wait, and slow down before attempting to return any ball, particularly those which rebound from the penthouse or the walls. The court tennis ball does not bounce very high — 18 to 24 inches being an average bounce — but there is a surprising amount of time for a player to get into position for a return. As a general rule, the player must be behind the ball, in a position to step forward into a shot. Only practice develops the powers of anticipation needed for this positioning. Then the player must learn how to turn on the smooth, coordinated, controlled power to make a successful return. It has been said that seven to ten years are needed to make a good court tennis player; this is probably not at all an exaggeration.

Courtesies

Court tennis still subscribes to high standards of sporting behavior. The game, played in its concrete enclosure where sounds bounce from walls and ceiling and words become difficult to understand because of the accoustics, is marked by quiet dignity. Scores are spoken, not shouted. Compliments are exchanged at the close of good play ("Well done! Well played!" "Thank you"). The gallery maintains a hush during rallies, muffling exclamations and saving applause for intervals between play.

One custom, taught early and scrupulously observed, requires the defender of a chase to enter the court first when sides are exchanged to play for the chase.

In announcing the score it is customary to name first the score of the winner of the last stroke.

Rules

Rule 1 of the "Laws of Tennis" deals with definitions of terms particular to court tennis. For example, "drop" refers to the ball's first bounce on the floor after it crosses the net. "Fall" refers to its second touch, and ends the play. A ball may also drop or fall into an opening. Chases are said to be "better than" or "worse than" marks on the floor.

Other rules describe choice of sides, chases, winning plays, and playing errors. Duties of the referee and marker are outlined.

Scoring in court tennis consists of four points for each game, known as "fifteen," "thirty," "forty," and "game." A score of zero is called "love." When both players have won three rallies (called "strokes" in the 1934 rule book), the score is called "deuce." The next stroke won by a player is scored "advantage" for that player. If the same person wins the next point, the game is won; if not the score goes back to deuce.

Games are gathered into "sets," the winner of the set to have six games. "Advantage" sets—that is, those requiring the winner to have a two game lead—are played only if the players agree, or in situations where odds are in use.

Court tennis has a handicapping system granting odds to less accomplished players, thus evening up the contest. Half odds and full odds, where certain strokes are given according to a set play, are most common. The "bisque" is another kind of handicapping where the receiver of the stroke may claim it on demand at almost any time in the game. "Cramped" odds refer to special deals where the game is cramped against the stronger player. Such provisions as "bar all openings," "bar the winning openings," "touch no side walls," or "touch no walls" can even up the game between the poorest matched opponents.

Rules for doubles play and play among three contestants are also described.

Professional Play

Professionalism, as applied to court tennis, refers to the teachers and coaches of the sport who are employed by the seven tennis courts in the United States and the 24 courts in England, the Continent, and Australia. Their main source of income derives from work directly connected with their places of employment and only incidentally with prize money.

A tennis pro has a good position and an exciting, challenging life, but the limited job opportunities are, of course, obvious.

Books and Periodicals

Available reading in court tennis, particularly in regard to description of the rules and how to play the game, is pitifully small. Most people are restricted to brief outlines found in encyclopedias, or occasional articles in periodicals. Books have appeared from time to time, but many are out of print and are not available in public libraries. The New York Racquet and Tennis Club is reputed to have one of the best collections known on court tennis, but this collection, seldom used even by the membership, is privately owned by the club library and unavailable to the public. Therefore, the few books mentioned are the only ones readily at hand at this time. (See the Bibliography.)

Organizations

The United States Court Tennis Association, Inc.
  John E. Slater, President
  McGraw-Hill Publications Co.
  1221 Ave of Americas
  New York NY 10020

The Tennis and Rackets Association
  The Queen's Club
  West Kensington, London, W14
  England

Chapter 2

Tennis

History

The origin of modern tennis goes directly back to 1873 when Walter Clopton Wingfield, a retired British cavalry major, introduced a game he called *sphairistiké* (from a Greek word meaning "to hit") to a group of friends in Nantclwyd, Wales. At this point, the conjecture begins. Was Wingfield independently wealthy or genteely poor? Was he an entrepreneur, scrambling to augment a dwindling income inherited from a well-bred family? Or was he merely seeking to amuse his friends, who were bored with croquet, by giving them a new game? Did he really claim to have found his game through research of ancient Greek archeological findings? Or did he finally admit to riding the crest of the vogue for anything tied to ancient Greek culture (a vogue heightened by Schliemann's impending excavation of Troy) and acknowledge inventing "tennis on the lawn" by blending elements of racquets, badminton, court tennis, English fives, and French *longue paume*?

It does not seem to matter now. What Wingfield did was to devise, promote, and package a game idea, apply for a patent and a copyright, and entice the players from the indoor courts and intricate laws of the dying court tennis onto the outdoor greens and simple rules of lawn tennis. (*Sphairistiké*, soon shortened to "sticky" by the game's detractors, never caught on as a name.)

Major Wingfield swung easily with the tide as the game's popularity grew. Graciously he allowed revisions and changes in the format, including court layout (soon abandoning a kind of hourglass court shape), net height (quickly lowered from a casual imitation of badminton's five feet), and scoring (replacing racquets scoring with an adaptation from court tennis). He seemed not to worry about the selection of a racquet, so long as people bought from him, and modelled his own on the court tennis "bat" as it was called. His primary control of the game lay in his letters patent and copyright, applied for and presumably granted in 1874. Through these he marketed a wooden chest containing racquets, rubber balls, wedges, pins, tape (for marking lines), and a hammer. Later it appears that a net or nets were added to the kit. Detailed rules of the game cost extra and could be ordered. French and Company, of Pimlico, London, was the supplier.

By 1875 Major Wingfield had established himself in what seemed like a position of monetary security and leadership in the emerging world of lawn tennis, but the surge in the game's popularity soon gathered the momentum to wash over and almost destroy him. As he prepared to publish an update of his rules, the All-England Croquet Club in Wimbledon set aside a fine lawn area to play lawn tennis. Spurred by the development of a new tennis ball (a hollow rubber ball covered with flannel and introduced the previous year), and goaded further by the need to find some activity to bail out the croquet club from imminent financial disaster, a tennis tournament was devised. "The Wimbledon" exists today as the synonym for prestigious world competition in tennis.

The success of this move is demonstrated by the fact that in 1877 the club name was changed to "All-England Croquet and Tennis Club" and earnest efforts were made to standardize Wingfield's scrambled and possibly plagiarized rules. Soon Wimbledon came of age. A game closely resembling modern tennis emerged. A subcommittee, organized that year to oversee the tournament, marked the beginning of formal tennis organization in England. Major Wingfield, now discredited and by-passed in the rush, was to be almost forgotten in the tennis world.

Meanwhile, tennis had reached the United States. Miss Mary Outerbridge, of Staten Island, N.Y., while vacationing in Bermuda early in 1874, saw the game played and was immediately captivated. She bought one of Major Wingfield's kits and imported it to the United States in February. The first game was played at the Staten Island Cricket and Baseball Club in New York. Soon her older brothers stepped in and took over developing the new sport. By 1880, Emelius Outerbridge had virtually assumed the lead in tennis promotion in the United States. The United States National Lawn Tennis Association was formed in 1881 in New York, with Outerbridge

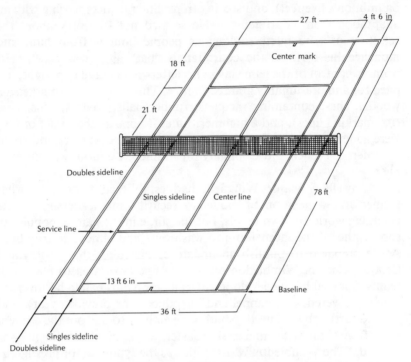

Diagram of tennis court.

as a member of the executive committee. The Davis Cup Tournament came along in 1900 with the first matches at Forest Hills, N.Y., followed by the Wightman Cup in 1923.

The United States Tennis Association, until 1975 entitled the United States Lawn Tennis Association, now comprises the governing body for the sport in America.

In the half century since the 1920s, tennis overwhelmed the world. It is without doubt the most popular individual sport; millions of people in almost all places and cultures now play the game. Literally thousands of books and articles are in print, covering every single aspect of the sport: history, teaching, coaching, biography, marketing—everything. The reader well may be baffled, often frustrated, in selecting from the mountainous array of information in trying to learn about the game.

The present book confines its discussion of tennis to basics—the fundamentals of the game as it is played today—and includes a selected list of books designed to help player and fan alike in exploring further. (See the Bibliography.)

The Game

Modern tennis is a robust sport requiring first of all dedication from anyone who would learn the game. The ability to move quickly, to start, stop and change direction smoothly, is basic to good play. Rhythm, timing, control, pace, strength, and endurance are also essential to success in tennis.

Tennis is played by two individuals (singles) or two couples (doubles) on a court measuring 27 feet by 78 feet for singles, 36 by 78 for doubles. Midway on the court length a net is stretched, measuring 3½ feet at the posts and three feet at the center of the court. Court markings include outer boundary lines and service court lines (see diagram) and are simple to understand.

Courts may be constructed indoors or outdoors, with surfaces of concrete, board, composition, dirt, clay or grass (the last being traditional to the game once formally known as "lawn tennis"). Most courts are laid down as doubles courts, for both singles and doubles games can be played on the larger court whereas the opposite is not true.

Play consists of striking a hollow, rubber, fabric-covered pressurized ball with a stringed racquet across a net in such a manner that the opposing team cannot make a legal return. In the course of each point the ball is "rallied" back and forth across the net until an error stops the play. Either the serving or the receiving side may score points. Details of tennis scoring appear later in the chapter.

Unlike most of the other sports described in this book, where the initial experience with a game provides enough success to give the beginner at least a glimpse of future fun, few newcomers to tennis show signs of instant expertise. Indeed, instant frustration is most common. It is an extremely difficult game to learn to play well. Many good coaches state that playing three to four times a week is minimal to improving skills, twice a week will maintain them, and any less play will result in their deterioration. (The amount of time spent by aspiring professionals is little less than astounding; schedules of seven to eight hours daily, seven days a week, are not at all unusual.) Furthermore, a player who would improve needs someone slightly more skilled for an opponent. In playing for fun, no great disparity should exist between skill levels, for games against a much better or much worse opponent usually result in little pleasure for anyone.

From the ready position, a player can move easily in any direction. Note the "shake hands" forehand grip, the one most often used. All white clothing, once de rigueur, has given way to a more informal approach.

Equipment

The racquet

The official rules have no specifications whatsoever in regard to a regulation tennis racquet. Indeed, not until rule 6 (Delivery of Service) does the word "racket" appear for the first time in the USTA "Rules of Tennis."

Most modern racquets measure 26½ to 27 inches in length, with a head width approximately 9½ inches. The grip usually varies from 4⅛ to 4¾ inches in circumference. Racquet weights are less than a pound, 13¼ ounces being an average figure for an aluminum racquet. There are also variations in the balance points of racquets, some being more heavy in the head than others.

The search for the perfect racquet goes on unceasingly. At present racquets are constructed of wood, fiberglass, graphite, steel, aluminum, and boron. Strings are nylon or gut, the latter being the usual choice of advanced players. Among brands currently advertised are the old timers of Wilson, Spalding, Bancroft, Davis, and Dunlop, now sharing the market with Head, Yamaha, Yonex, Garcia, Aldila, PDP, Donnay, Adidas, Kawasaki, Hanson, Pancho Segura, Groves-Kelco, Dura Fiber, Slazenger, Maxply Fort, Rawlings, and Fischer. The Elaine Mason is a racquet claiming 50% larger head size and designed for regular play. Extra-length racquets have appeared from time to time, but no players have come along to control the longer length. One so-called "wonder-racket," designed by Werner Fischer of West Germany, has caused great discussion among top players. A unique system of strings, in which some are doubled and small plastic tubes are used to join vertical and horizontal strings, is said to bring unpredictable spin to the ball and increase the speed of the serve. It has even been reported that a few federations have banned the use of this racquet, but an official rules change has not been made.

Therefore, the player can look to the teaching pro, the pocket book, and individual preference in trying to choose the "right" racquet. The basic guideline always comes down to what the player believes gives the best results.

The ball

Specifications for size, weight, and bound of the regulation tennis ball are meticulously outlined in the official rules. In general the

The server stands behind the baseline, to the right or left of the center marker, for service delivery. Two balls are normally held for convenient redelivery of service if the first effort results in a fault. There is a great sense of exhilaration in a well-hit serve.

ball measures slightly larger than 2½ inches in diameter, weighs just above two ounces, and is white or yellow or orange with stitchless seams. Specifications are also given for bounce and deformation. Pressurized balls are now standard for play; nonpressurized and low-pressure balls need formal agreement for the International Tennis Championships (Davis Cup), for example.

Balls listed in the USTA Yearbook, as approved for sanctioned matches for 1977, include the following brands: A.W. Phillips, Bancroft (Tretorn), Dunlop, Fred Perry, Garcia, Goodall, MacGregor, Nassau, Penn, Pancho Gonzales, Slazenger, Spalding, Wilson, and Wingfield.

Clothing

No regulation for clothing appears in the USTA rules; selection is based on comfort and tradition. White, once considered *de rigueur* in tennis, now shares honors with all colors. (Indeed, even tennis courts used in television play are now laid down in color blocks rather than as mere lines painted on a single colored suface.) In general, players select lightweight fabrics and abbreviated costume for regular tennis play.

Shoes, of course, are at the top of the priority list in tennis clothing. Once again, the player faces a bewildering variety of models from which to choose. Current advertisers in *Tennis Magazine* include Converse, Adidas, Tretorn, Fred Perry, Pro-Keds, Kacpa, Puma, Prima, K-Swiss, Tred-2, Uniroyal, Bata Polymatch, Head and Footjoy. Once more, the choice is up to the player.

Play of the Ball

The ball is put in play by the server who stands behind the baseline, tosses the ball in the air, and strikes it with the racquet so that it lands in the service court diagonal to the server. The receiver now returns the ball, which must cross the net before bouncing. From this point the ball may be volleyed (struck before bouncing), or played after the first bounce until an error or an unreturnable shot ends the play.

Experienced players use a variety of strokes, some of them unnecessary for the beginner but all of them important in some degree to the highly advanced player. These were categorized by Billie Jean King in the book, *Tennis to Win* (Harper & Row, New York, 1970) as ground strokes (i.e., those taken after the bounce), serves, volleys, overheads, and trimmings (lob, half volley, drop shot, drop volley, low volley). The recent popularity of the "big game" style of play (a strong serve followed by a rush to the net for a killing volley), demonstrates that the strictly baseline player has trouble against this form of play. However, since the serve alternates between singles players and doubles teams, mastery of baseline skills is still basic to the sport.

The present book will treat the following: forehand drive, backhand drive, two-handed backhand, serve, volley, lob, and overhead.

Fundamentals

Eastern, Western, and Continental are names traditionally used to describe most basic tennis grips. Each has been successful for great players of the sport, but the Eastern grip has emerged as one most often used and most often taught. The racquet is held in a conventional handshake grip with the lower edge of the racquet pointing to the court and the face of the racquet perpendicular. The hand is well spread along the grip, the forefinger curled in an extended position to give more control. Because the racquet is long and heavy, the hand is placed well up on the grip—not a "choked" position, yet one which allows the heel of the grip to extend a bit past the heel of the hand.

Forehand drive

In the flat forehand stroke (the one giving no spin on the ball), the right-handed player addresses the ball with the left side of the body turned toward the target, weight well back on the right foot, knees bent, both feet on the court, and arm well back. The feet are wide apart, generally parallel or in a slightly open position (i.e., the left foot may be several inches to the left of center), the wrist firm and extended, not cocked. The stroke is executed with a full arm sweep; the weight shifts from right foot to left as the arm moves, the shift being complete at the moment of impact; and the follow-through finishes the movement. The racquet moves roughly parallel to the court, or from a moderately low to high position. Many players find it helpful to think of the racquet face as a mere extension of the palm of the hand.

At the moment of impact, the ball is met squarely just about opposite the left toe. The racquet must be firmly held, the stroke devoid of wristy moves. The player's eyes must concentrate on the ball.

The mirror image of these techniques describes the left-handed player's approach to each stroke.

Backhand drive

The Eastern, or handshake, grip is shifted slightly by turning the racquet face in a clockwise direction so that the top edge of the racquet is positioned toward the target. Another way to describe this

Opposite: The forehand drive.

shift is to say that the hand rotates about an inch or more in a counter-clockwise direction. As the ball approaches, the right side is now turned toward it, the feet are in a definitely closed position and wide apart, knees are bent, the arm is back across the body, and the weight is on the left foot.

In executing the stroke, the player makes the weight transfer by stepping toward the net with the right foot. On impact the ball is met farther toward the net than in the forehand — approximately the width of the player's shoulders. The follow-through completes the stroke.

The two-handed backhand

The success of such players as Chris Evert and Bjorn Borg with the two-handed backhand has generated great interest in this stroke. It is far too early in the game to predict if this is a skill attainable only by a few, a real breakthrough in a basic skill, or a problematical teaching aid causing both confusion and triumph among the tennis learners of the world.

The advantages of the two-handed stroke lie in its increased power, its ease of control, and its help in teaching small, young players to handle the tennis racquet. The disadvantages lie in its shortened reach and its limited use in returning high and low balls. If a player is quick enough to make up for at least a half step lost by this short-ened reach and seems to have a natural aptitude for the stroke, there seems to be no reason not to continue developing it. But even though the stroke is rather freely taught, most players should probably spend their time learning the traditional backhand, with its more natural rhythm and longer reach.

The serve

Once the beginner is ready to progress from "patting" the ball into play, the first serve learned is usually the "slice." For this, a backhand grip is used, which will cause the racquet to move across the ball on contact, thus imparting spin to the ball.

The player stands behind the baseline, feet parallel to each other but at an angle oblique to the net, body slightly open to the net,

Opposite: The backhand drive. The racquet is rotated an inch or so counter-clockwise in the grip (for right-handers; oppositely for left-handers) — that is, the hand is more "on top" of the handle than in the forehand.

The two-handed backhand, a new and rather controversial stroke: correct rotation of the hips during the follow-through is a must. (Courtesy Valley Pioneer, Danville, Calif.; photo by Brent Bowen.)

weight on the left foot. The ball is tossed slightly to the right of the body and forward of the baseline to a height just beyond the reach of the player's extended racquet. As the ball is tossed, weight transfers to the right foot, the racquet head is brought behind the back, the right elbow is bent and pointing upward toward the ball. On execution the racquet head is snapped to the ball with strong wrist action. Contact with the ball is at full arm extension. The follow-through is across the body. In the course of the arm action, the weight transfers from the right foot to the left, being full on the left at the moment of impact. The server steps into the court with the right foot on the follow-through.

Players who have the strength and agility to play the "big" net-rushing game often use the slice serve for a second serve, substituting

Low and high volleys require different stances and intense concentration on the ball.

the flat or "cannon ball" for the first serve (see Rules — The serve, below, for first and second serve). The "American twist" is another popular serve for the advanced player, demanding great strength and perfect timing. Neither of these advanced serves is within the scope of this book.

The volley

A degree of volleying skill is necessary for any well-rounded tennis game, be it singles or doubles. Without competency in volleying, the doubles player in particular is greatly hampered.

Most volleys are taken near the net. For this shot the grip can be much the same as for forehand and backhand. The stroke itself is little more than bringing the racquet head up and into position to meet the ball firmly, with a minimum of swing, the action being like a push. The speed of the approaching ball results in a strong rebound from the racquet strings so that the volleyer need give little impetus to the ball.

Quick, crisp racquet placement, combined with a strong sense of anticipation, is the key to success in the volley. Often there is no time to be precise about footwork, but when there is, the general facings for forehand and backhand are used.

The lob

Generally a defensive stroke in tennis, the lob is most often used to force an opponent from an attacking position at the net. The stroke is executed by swinging the racquet in a low to high arc, with the racquet face open at the moment of impact. Success with the lob is dependent upon developing a sense of control and touch.

The overhead

This stroke is used to return a lob when the timing is such that a player can get into position to set up for the "kill." The moves are almost identical to those used in the serve. The overhead may be played either before or after the ball bounces. The stroke requires a keen sense of timing, intense concentration on the ball, and great confidence.

Courtesies

The modern game of tennis is witnessing an erosion of courtesies once so traditional to the game that they were like unwritten rules. Quiet during play, polite applause and restrained calls of praise at the end of an outstanding rally, and absence of booing all once characterized the behavior of the typical tennis gallery. On the part of the player, display of ill nature on the court, disputing official calls, obvious response to gallery moods, and unsporting use of what some call "gamesmanship" were scrupulously avoided. The player who ignored these courtesies, while providing colorful copy for the media, sacrificed the respect of other players. A noisy fan was kept in check by the gallery itself through discreet shushing.

Most players and fans still subscribe to these standards of sporting behavior, but less dignified actions are becoming more and more

Opposite, left: The lob needs a sense of touch, finesse, and confidence. Right: The foot fault, a far too common error, results from carelessness or inattention to the rules.

tolerated, even accepted. With the tremendous increase in the number of players and fans, it is reasonable to forecast a continued drift toward total informality. Just how far it will go is, to be sure, anybody's guess.

Rules

The following remarks may be construed only as a commentary on, or paraphrase of, official rules of the game. Current rules may be purchased from the USTA (address at the end of the chapter), and are also often distributed free by tennis centers, sporting goods stores, and manufacturers of tennis equipment.

The serve

The serve is decided by toss. The ball is delivered at the beginning of each game from the righthand side of the court, then alternates between right and left for each succeeding delivery throughout the game. In singles the same person serves for one game, becoming the receiver for the ensuing game. In doubles the serve also changes at the end of each game, from one team to the other, each individual serving in rotation for one game.

The server has two chances on each serve to make a proper delivery. Faulty serves occur if the ball fails to clear the net, if the ball lands outside the prescribed service area, or if the server commits a foot fault (placing a foot inside the court before hitting the ball). A properly delivered ball which touches the net on the way to the correct court is called a "let" and served over.

Return of service

When the receiver returns the ball, it must cross the net to the opponent's court before it may be played. The ball may be volleyed or allowed to bounce. It is now rallied, or in play, until an error is made or an unreturnable shot ends the play. Errors include hitting the ball into the net, sending the ball out-of-bounds, failing to return the ball before the second bounce, or touching the net with racquet or body. An unreturnable shot is simply one so well placed that the opponent cannot play it.

Scoring

Either the serving or the receiving side may score points. The lowest scoring unit in tennis is the point. Points are accumulated to form a *game*, games to form a *set*, and sets to make a *match*. A score of zero is called "love." Games consist of four points called "fifteen," "thirty," "forty," and "game," with a special provision for scoring should the score be tied at "forty-all." In this instance, the score is called "deuce." It is then called "advantage" to the team that wins the next point. Should the team at advantage win the *next* point also, the game is won. Should it lose, the score reverts to deuce, and so on until the team at advantage wins the point and the game.

A set is completed when six games are won, including a two game margin. Should play be tied at five-all, the score "6-5" is not considered to be a complete set. Play must continue until one team has a two-game lead. In tournament play, tie breakers may be used for sets that are tied, usually at six-all. Matches are the best two out of three or three out of five sets.

Tie breakers

Tie breakers have long been discussed in tennis circles. It was not until the arrival of television, however, with its need for firm time allotments in game coverage, that tie breakers received official sanction. Traditionally, the rules of the game have always evolved slowly. The long, drawn-out deuce-advantage games and lengthy sets, for so many years both the delight and the despair of tennis fans and players, do not fit expensive television programming or the tastes of the viewing public. No sponsor could afford to show a match such as the one between Jaroslav Drobny and Budge Patty in 1953 — a contest lasting five hours and consisting of a total of 91 games in five sets. And although history calls it a "true battle of the giants," few modern tennis buffs would sit through such a match. At least, so goes current thinking. Thus, the advent of the tie breaker.

There is no denying that the use of tie breakers changes the nature of the sport. But their almost universal acceptance demonstrates the complete capitulation to our speeded-up life style as well as how commercialism is forcing changes on once traditional games. Endless discussions have ensued, weighing the good against the bad of tie breakers, but they are probably here to stay.

The Wimbledon Tie Breaker, sanctioned for use in ILTF tournaments, is a 7-of-12-point tie breaker. When the set ties at six-all, the first player to win seven points wins the set. Special rules for serving and receiving order are outlined for both doubles and singles play.

The 5-of-9 is the most common tie breaker used in tournament play. The "broken" set is recorded as seven games to six.

Another method for speeding play is the VASSS "No-Ad" scoring. (The initials stand for Van Alen Simplified Scoring System.) As the "No-Ad" implies, the score beyond deuce goes to "game" rather than "advantage." Any experienced tennis player will affirm that this changes the nature of the game drastically. It is still hotly debated, special authorization being needed from the ILTF for its use by any ILT sanctioned tournament.

Timed matches have also been tried, using another form of VASSS. These have generally met with little favor from both players and spectators.

Competitive Play

Amateur

With an estimated 34,000,000 weekend players in the United States alone, the opportunities for amateur play are boundless. Two recent publications show the degree and depth of competition today. The *Tennis Yearbook* (an annual official publication of the USTA), has over 500 pages devoted to administration of the sport, covering such aspects as committees, playing season, player rankings, section organizations, championships, past records, international results and records, and official rules of the game. It is an important resource for any tennis player.

Another publication, the *Official United States Tournament Directory*, made its first appearance for the 1977-1978 season. Its over 250 pages deal solely with tournaments scheduled in the 50 states and the District of Columbia. It carries national listings, tournament locations, and entry procedures for amateur and professional circuits — juniors, adults, and seniors — well over 1200 events. Also included are dates, locations, and prize money for the major professional circuits.

Professional Tennis

In 1926, Charles C. Pyle, a promoter known as "Cash and

Carry Pyle," offered $50,000 to the French star, Suzanne Lenglen, to tour the United States. Vincent Richards, Harvey Snodgrass, Howard O. Kinsey (of the United States) and Paul Peret (of France) were induced to accompany the tour as paid players. The outstanding success of this venture gave direct impetus to the founding of the United States Professional Lawn Tennis Association in 1927 by Richards and Kinsey. Twenty years later, in 1947, Jack Kramer, winner at Wimbledon and three time Davis Cup member, moved into playing, promotion, and management of professional tennis for the express purpose of bringing it into a position of honor and status in the tennis world. Through his move, "power tennis" or "the big game" came of age. Now the world has amateur, open, and professional tennis. World Championship Tennis represents the top of the professional pyramid. There appears to be no limit to the opportunities for earning a living as a tennis player, from generous college scholarships to five-figured salaried contracts plus prize money. All that is required of the would-be professional tennis player is enormous talent and tremendous capacity for hard work.

Organizations (major)

Association of Intercollegiate Athletics for Women (AIAW)
    1201 16th St NW
    Washington DC 20036

Association of Tennis Professionals (ATP)
    Box 581
    Dallas TX 75207

National Collegiate Athletic Association (NCAA)
    Shawnee Mission KS 66322

National Junior College Athletic Association (NJCAA)
    12 E 2nd St
    Hutchinson KS 67501

United States Professional Tennis Association (USPTA)
    6701 Highway 58
    Harrison TN 37341
    (Publishes *Tennis; The Magazine of the Racquet Sports*)

United States Tennis Association (USTA)
   51 E 42nd St
   New York NY 10011
   (Publishes *Tennis Yearbook, U.S. Tennis Tournament Directory*,
     and *Official Rules of Lawn Tennis*

World Championship Tennis
   1990 First National Bank Bldg
   Dallas TX 75202

Chapter 3

Platform Tennis

History

Platform tennis has been popular on the East Coast of the United States since the mid 1930s. It owes much to its antecedent, paddle tennis, a game still played throughout the country. Even now, players of both platform tennis and paddle tennis often refer to their sport as "paddle." Some sporting goods manufacturers still fail to distinguish between the games, apparently believing that the official platform tennis ball and the official paddle tennis ball are one and the same. (They are not.) The fact that the same paddles are used for both sports adds to the confusion, particularly for nonplayers. Individuals who decide to take up either paddle tennis or platform tennis are cautioned to be sure to know which game they are seeking.

The first paddle tennis game was invented by the Rev. Frank P. Beal. As a boy in Albion, Michigan, in 1898, he devised a miniature tennis game that could be played on a 39 by 18 foot court, a space half the size of one side of a regulation doubles tennis court. He made a small wooden paddle to serve as a racquet and used a spongy rubber ball which would not fly quite so fast or far as a tennis ball.

In 1921, Mr. Beal, then associate minister of Judson Memorial Church in Greenwich Village, adapted his boyhood game to the city streets, gymnasium floors, and flat playground spaces of New York while attempting to solve a serious recreation problem. He thought of the game as a lead-up to tennis and especially good for children. Tennis stars Bobby Riggs, Althea Gibson, and Pancho Gonzales all got their starts in the game playing paddle tennis as children.

43

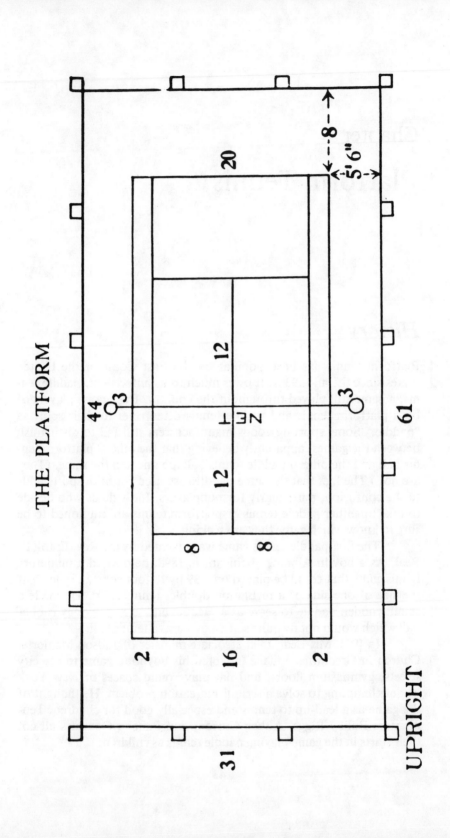

THE PLATFORM

UPRIGHT

20

12

12

8

8

2

16

2

31

3

3

44

61

N
E
T

5'6"

8

The Evans Backstop forms an essential part of a properly constructed platform tennis court.

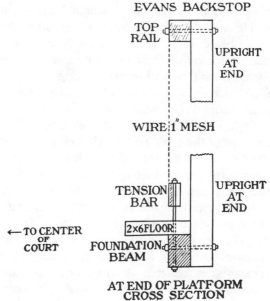

EVANS BACKSTOP

TOP RAIL

UPRIGHT AT END

WIRE 1" MESH

TENSION BAR

UPRIGHT AT END

← TO CENTER OF COURT

2×6 FLOOR

FOUNDATION BEAM

AT END OF PLATFORM
CROSS SECTION

Organization to standardize competition dates back to 1923 when leading proponents of the game formed the American Paddle Tennis Association. The name was changed in 1926 to its present name: the United States Paddle Tennis Association. (The initials USPTA also designate the United States Professional Tennis Association, an unfortunate coincidence.) Eight years later, in 1934, a new game, the one now known as platform tennis, formed its own association. For reasons now difficult to understand, the name, "American *Paddle* Tennis Association" (italics added) was selected, with the knowledge and permission of the USPTA. Not until 1950 did the platform tennis leaders substitute "platform" for "paddle" in the name and give their formal organization its more accurate designation: the American Platform Tennis Association.

But the confusion between both the sports and their governing bodies was by then well engrained and may be here to stay. Nowadays only the players and the fans of the respective sports understand for certain which game their organizations represent. And, of course, as an outgrowth of this confusion as much as anything else, there was and still is rivalry between the sports, not all of it friendly.

The younger game, platform tennis, was invented by Fessenden S. Blanchard and James K. Cogswell in 1928. These two men were ten-

Opposite: The layout of a platform tennis court.

nis enthusiasts, residents of Scarsdale, N.Y., and in those days of clay and lawn, before the development of indoor tennis courts, they fretted miserably during the long months when winter weather ended the playing season of their favorite game. They decided to build a platform on a bit of land owned by Cogswell, coming up with a 48 by 20 foot deck on which they hoped to play volleyball, deck tennis, or badminton. When winter winds made these games unsuitable, they thought of paddle tennis and tried it out. Tired of chasing balls down the edge of the bank over which their platform was built, they enclosed their space with wire mesh. Soon they found that by allowing rebounds to be played from the wire fence (after first having bounced on the court and before touching the court again), the game became more balanced and more fun. Smashes and kills, common winning shots, no longer overpowered the game. They allowed only one service attempt per point, again creating more balance between server and receiver. The court was somewhat enlarged, the height of the net and screens standardized. A great advance came along in 1934 when Donald K. Evans, also of Scarsdale, designed the Evans Backstop: a device for suspending and stretching the one inch wire mesh in such a way as to give a uniform bounce for screen play. (See diagram.) And finally, a standard ball, heavier and mushier than a tennis ball, was produced for regular play.

The first club courts were constructed at the prestigious Fox Meadow Tennis Club in Scarsdale and met with instantaneous enthusiasm by tennis players.

As platform tennis grew modestly in popularity, paddle tennis boomed, spurred by government aid in developing massive recreation centers throughout the entire United States during the Depression. For a while it appeared that the platform game would remain an exclusive sport, limited to the wealthy and to the country club, while the older game would maintain everlasting popularity on the playground.

Murray Geller, president of the United States Paddle Tennis Association, writes in *Paddle Tennis, Official Rules and Answers*:

"With the passage of time, interest in the children's game (paddle tennis) waned. The original court and rules had built-in weaknesses which inevitably led to the virtual demise of the 39 by 18 foot court. As players improved their overhead serves and rushed the net, it was almost impossible to lob against these net rushers on the short court. There were hardly any rallies; it was essentially a game of slamming. Nearly all the courts in the New York City and Los Angeles Park and Recreation Department's playgrounds eventually fell into disuse and disrepair.

"The exciting paddle tennis renaissance began in January, 1959, with the nationwide publication of the radical, contemporary United States Paddle Tennis Association Rules, court dimensions, and unique court markings. The adoption of the one underhand serve, tennis ball punctured to deaden its bounce, 2 foot 7 inch taut net, 3 foot lob area rule, larger court (50 feet by 20 feet), and the one bounce rule for singles have made contemporary paddle tennis a fast, furious and spectacular sport with prolonged rallies and a premium on agility. Paddle tennis is no longer a children's game."

Platform tennis, meanwhile, developed steadily without the lag of its parent sport. From an East Coast winter sport, it spread across the nation to the West Coast and is now played in all seasons. There is apparently room for both kinds of "paddle." The present book has chosen the more recent game, platform tennis, for discussion in this chapter. Paddle tennis is described in the chapter on Playground Games.

The Game

Control is the basic ingredient of platform tennis, combined with concentration, quick reaction time, and clever, strategic adaptations to sudden changes of pace. The game is played in its most popular form by four players (two on a side) on an outdoor, rectangular, screened-in platform. The playing surface measures 20 feet by 44 feet and is surrounded by a 12 foot wire fence, 31 feet wide and 61 feet long. (See diagram.) Court markings closely resemble those of a tennis court and are, in fact, but scaled down to a smaller court size. The net measures 37 inches at the posts and 34 inches at the center.

Play consists of striking a small spongy ball with a paddle across a low net in such a way that the opposing team cannot make a legal return. In the course of play the ball is rallied back and forth across the net until an error stops the play. Either the serving side or the receiving side may win points. The scoring is identical to tennis.

Most platform tennis courts are built on raised platforms, the playing surfaces having originally been made of wooden planks placed slightly apart to aid in melting snow run-off. Hinged side boards at the bottom of the fence are for snow removal. Modern courts now use metal "planks" or, where snow is no problem, are constructed directly on the ground, using more traditional surfacing. The hinged boards remain for ease in court maintenance. Lighting for night play is placed along the tops of the side fences and is standard equipment in new court construction.

The public platform tennis courts at College of Notre Dame, Belmont, Calif. Note the lights along the fence tops and the movable gates along the fence bottoms. The gates are for leaf sweeping and snow removal. Three courts can be built in the space of one full sized tennis court.

Platform tennis offers almost instant success to beginners, regardless of age and racquet sports experience. Fundamental strokes are easily mastered. Singles play (one player on each side) is excellent experience for learning the game, getting a good practice workout, and developing strokes, but as players become more skillful, only doubles offers real challenge and excitement in competitive play.

Builders and installers of platform tennis courts advertise in *Paddle World*, the monthly platform tennis magazine. Names as well as official rules of the game can be obtained from the American Platform Tennis Association. Sanctioned events are all men's or women's doubles and mixed doubles, singles competition at the national level having been discontinued in 1938.

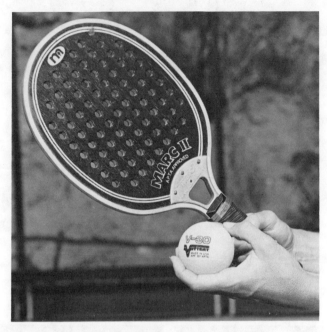

The platform tennis ball is unique to the game. The paddle is used in both platform tennis and paddle tennis.

Equipment

The paddle

The usual platform tennis paddle is made from maple, weighs between 13 and 16 ounces, and measures approximately 17 inches overall. The paddle face is roughly oval, about 8¼ by 10 inches. The face is perforated with small holes, which reduce wind resistance and provide the hitter more control. A leather wrist thong is optional.

The regulation paddle is not mandated in the rules. Experiments are in progress using materials such as aluminum, fiber glass, and plastics. Presumably other sizes and shapes of paddles will some day be used. However, at present, the wooden paddle is most popular. Experiments with stringed racquets have failed to take hold in the game, chiefly because the strings totally destroy the characteristics of the game. ("It just isn't paddle," is the usual comment.) Dalton, F.L. Fiberglass, Sportcraft, Vittery, Dunlop, and Marcraft currently manufacture paddles, and the list is growing.

The backhand sequence

The ball

An unpressurized sponge rubber ball, approximately 2½ inches in diameter (slightly smaller than a tennis ball), is regulation for the game. Orange is the most popular color although balls are available in white and yellow. Distributors include Marcraft, Eagle Rubber, Sports Beconta, General Sportcraft, Bullet, and Barr.

Clothing

The official rules of platform tennis do not specify official clothing but the nature of the game requires some kind of tennis shoes. The abrasive quality of eastern court surfaces and the quick starts and stops in all play make the "best" footwear a problem yet to be

Opposite: The forehand sequence. The handshake grip answers both forehand and backhand needs.

solved. Sports Beconta and Uniroyal Pro-Keds and Petriak Athletic Shoe advertise special platform tennis shoes, some with extra protection around the toe, a durable sole, and a slightly higher back.

Clothing for platform tennis resembles tennis wear in mild climates and extremely casual, outdoor ice skating attire where weather is cold. Easterners, when playing in midwinter, often start the game dressed in layers of clothing. As the competitors warm up, the layers are peeled off to turtle neck sweaters and slacks while spectators or those next on the court wait and watch from the warming shed. Longtime platform tennis players prefer this lack of standardization in dress.

Play of the Ball

The ball is put in play at the start of each point by the server, who stands behind the baseline, tosses the ball in the air, and strikes it. The ball must cross the net and land in the service court diagonal to the server. The server has only one chance per point to make a proper delivery. Each game starts from the righthand court, the service then alternating to the left, then the right, and so on throughout the game. The same player delivers the service for the whole game.

The receiver must allow the served ball to bounce before returning it. The ball is now rallied back and forth, across the net, until one side or another commits an error. Either the serving or receiving side may earn points.

After the return of service, the ball may now be volleyed (returned before bouncing), struck after one bounce, or hit on a rebound from the screen. The latter occurs when a legally returned ball strikes the court surface within the legal marking lines, then strikes the screened fence. The player trying to return the ball may play on this ricochet before or after it touches the court surface. A ball may not be hit directly from court to screen. It must first take a legal (in bounds) bounce.

Strokes used in platform tennis are similar to traditional tennis strokes and are easily borrowed and adapted from it. The serve is similar to tennis, being generally overhand. The lob can be the backbone of a good platform tennis game, coupled with drives and angled shots; but for many players the volley, used both as an approach and as a net shot, forms the heart of the game. The overhead is another shot often used in platform tennis. The unique strokes are found in those where the ball is played off the wire screens.

Fundamentals

Forehand

In the forehand the paddle is held in a traditional handshake grip used in most racquet sports: edge of the paddle pointing to the court, faces of the paddle perpendicular. Many players shift the grip slightly counterclockwise, allowing the top of the paddle to lean a bit forward (a closed position), thus putting top spin on each stroke. These two grips appear to be standard, a matter of individual preference. In both grips the hand is well spread along the handle with forefinger curled in an extended position for more control.

The forehand stroke forms the basis for most hits in platform tennis. It is executed much like the forehand in the larger tennis game, but is shorter, more circumscribed, and tightly controlled. For the right-handed player the body is turned so that the left side is toward the target, knees bent, paddle back and high, weight on the right foot. The stroke is executed with a brief arm-sweep, the weight shifts to the left foot at the moment of impact, and the follow-through completes the movement. The contact is firm and not at all "wristy." Controlled spin may be added to a more sophisticated forehand by a slight forearm roll on impact. The ball is met just opposite or a bit forward of the left toe.

The left-handed player's approach is the mirror image of these techniques. Intense concentration on the ball, complete to the moment of impact, is basic to consistent success in all platform tennis strokes.

Backhand

Shifting the grip from the forehand stroke to a special backhand grip appears to be a matter of individual preference in this game. If the grip is changed, the hand moves an inch or two clockwise on the handle, and the top of the paddle face slants toward the target (an open position). As the ball approaches, the player's right side is now toward it, the paddle back across the body, the weight on the left foot. In executing the stroke, the player transfers the weight to the right foot, synchronizing this change with the swing. On impact, the paddle face is perpendicular to the court or slightly open, the follow-through high. Although the backhand is not used so often as the forehand, it is an indispensable stroke, particularly valuable in playing certain shots off the wire screens.

Forehand and backhand volleys both require precision in paddle placement and very little impact on the ball.

The volley

Because doubles has developed into the most exciting form of platform tennis, it is of utmost importance for the player to develop the volley. The shot requires a stiff wrist and a tight grip. The stroke is a short, punched shot, using no more than a half swing. Generally the return should be low and tightly controlled. High bouncing returns will reach the wire screen and may be successfully returned whereas low bouncing, sharply angled volleys are point winners.

The volley may be used effectively from midcourt to net position, the first being an "approach" volley, the second a "net" volley. (The approach volley is made possible because the half-court length is less than 32 feet.) Clever anticipation of the opposing team's ball placement, quick reaction time, and precise control give the team in volleying position a decided edge. Players who come to platform tennis from tennis often find their net games dramatically improved when they return to the big tennis court.

The lob

In platform tennis, the lob has unique versatility in that it can be either an offensive or defensive shot. It is also the shot most frequently used in retrieving a ball from the screen.

Both the forehand and the backhand lobs are executed with a stroke that travels from low to high. Knees are well bent at the start of the swing. The paddle face is frankly open on impact. The ball is met further back than in the other strokes. Control and a sense of touch are the keys to a good lob.

The overhead

Generally played near the net, this shot requires great forebearance from the player who likes to smash or slam an overhead. A hard hit will often carom from a screen and set up an easy return.

In the overhand stroke, the ball is contacted high and in front of the player. The stroke is executed much like the service, including a wrist cock and straightening at the moment of impact, but with less time for its performance.

The serve

Control once more forms the basis for this stroke, adapted and modified from the big tennis serve, for the platform tennis player gets only one chance to put the ball in play (rather than two, as in tennis). The grip varies from beginner to skilled player, ultimately becoming a matter of personal choice. In general, the grip resembles that used for the forehand.

The right-handed player stands with the left side toward the net, weight on the left foot. The ball is tossed upward and forward (toward the net). As the ball is tossed, the weight moves over the right foot. The paddle head drops back behind the right shoulder, the wrist cocks. At execution the weight moves forward to the left foot, the paddle head is thrown or snapped to meet the ball at the fullest extension of the arm. Follow-through is toward the net and usually accompanied by the right foot stepping in that direction.

The beginner usually "pats" the ball into play, but since the "big serve" carries little premium in platform tennis, it is not hard for any player to develop a good, ego-satisfying serve.

Screen shots (balls taken after a rebound from the fence) depend on timing and concentration for success.

Screen shots

The trickiest part of playing rebounds from the wire deals with timing. The beginner finds that there is much more time available for the stroke than at first appears. Also, the ball will fly farther away from the screen than one may think it will. With practice the player learns to take a position well out from the place where the ball meets the screen, to wait (put on the brakes, so to speak) before starting the stroke, then to move. In general the paddle head follows the ball well after the rebound and meets it with a lifting action.

The screen shot is unique to platform tennis. The comment is often made by people who have never seen the game and who are trying to visualize the shot, "it's like squash or racquetball." This is completely inaccurate. The change of tempo from quick shifting about the court in nonscreen play to the controlled, stop-action wait for the rebound adds an exciting fillip to the game, a timing found in but one other racquet sport: court tennis, a game few platform tennis players have ever seen.

Scoring

The platform tennis scoring is identical to tennis. Games consist of four points called "fifteen," "thirty," "forty," and "game," with special provision should the game be tied at "forty-all." In this instance the score is called "deuce." It is then called "advantage" for the team that wins the next point. Should the team at advantage win the next point, the game is won. Should it lose, the score reverts to deuce, and so on until the team at advantage wins the point and the game.

The score of zero is called "love."

Games are grouped into "sets." A set is won when a team wins six games, including a two game margin. Should play be tied at five-all, the score "6-5" is not considered to be a complete set. The play must continue until one team has a two game lead. In tournament play, tie-breakers are often used for sets tied at six-all to save time. (See chapter on tennis.)

Courtesies

The inventors of platform tennis brought with them the traditions and courtesies of tennis but without some of the old-fashioned stuffiness which once infused the game of tennis. (For example, the player's attire may be extremely casual.) Although the game is often sociably noisy, squabbles over controversial calls and ill-natured behavior are rare. During match play spectators remain quiet; the players perform with intense concentration. Handshakes and compliments are exchanged at the end of the matches, and the "wait till next time" comments are given with good feeling.

Rules

The official rules state that unless otherwise noted, the rules of the United States Tennis Association apply. These notations include:

    playing balls off the screen

    only one serve

    rules for balls which bounce over the fence

    foot fault rules

Some sporting goods stores carry rules of the game. The official guides may be obtained by writing the American Platform Tennis Association.

As a lead-up to tennis, the platform game has no equal. This boy is not yet five.

Professional Platform Tennis

Organized professional play had its official start in 1975 with the formation of the American Professional Platform Tennis Association. The professional circuit began in Cleveland, Ohio, in December, 1975, culminating in the finals of the Tribuno World Platform Tennis Championship on April 3, 1976, at the famed Center Court of the West Side Tennis Club in Forest Hills, N.Y. (It is interesting to note that one platform tennis court contractor, in a recent leaflet promoting platform construction, referred to this event as the World *Paddle* Championship—italics added—again taking the name which confuses this sport with paddle tennis.)

Two full-sized platform tennis courts (temporary, semiportable), were constructed for the hundreds who filled much of the traditional tennis gallery. Enthusiastic platform tennis players and fans accurately regarded this as a major breakthrough for the sport and the start of an annual tradition. Beginning in 1977, the tour's new sponsor,

Calvert-Seagram, adopted the name "The Passport Tour of Platform Tennis" and granted thousands of dollars in prize money.

As professional and amateur interest grows, both players and coaches are realizing that initial playing experience on the platform is an excellent way to learn tennis, hence a movement toward building platform courts in conjunction with traditional tennis courts is under way and gathering momentum. Children and beginners alike receive immeasurable value from mastering platform tennis strokes and strategy before attempting the frustrations of tennis. Experienced tennis players who have discovered "paddle" now return to the platform for work on the volley and for just plain fun. They have discovered that the games complement rather than impair each other. Furthermore, the dedicated tennis player whose property does not have room for a court now finds that a platform will satisfy many needs and that a full sized platform court can be built on a fraction of the land required for a tennis court and for less than half the cost.

The practicality as well as monetary profit from adding platform facilities to tennis complexes has opened new professional doors. Courts constructed for club use include bleachers for spectators and lights for extended playing time, therebye attracting large and, of course, paying audiences. Demand for good equipment is growing. Magazine articles now appear in general sports publications. Television and newspapers cover important matches. Sponsors of professional events provide prize money and promotional services.

In light of the foregoing, it appears that there are several ways of earning good livings in the sport, including that of the professional player.

Organizations

American Platform Tennis Association
  52 Upper Montclair Plaza
  Upper Montclair NJ 07043
  Gloria Dillenbeck, Executive Secretary

American Professional Platform Tennis Association
  527 E 72d St
  New York NY 10021
  Linda Russell, Executive Secretary

United States Paddle Tennis Association
  c/o Murray Geller
  189 Seeley St
  Brooklyn NY 11218

Magazines

Paddle World (published quarterly)
Racquet and Paddle Publications, Inc.
370 Seventh Ave
New York NY 1001

Table tennis (see new chapter at right) is a game for all ages. Early in his career this player has learned to impart spin to his forehand.

Chapter 4
Table Tennis

History

Table tennis, like lawn tennis, had its recognizable start toward the close of the 19th century — recognizable, that is to say, in terms of the game as now played in the basements, attics, patios, and recreation rooms of millions of people all over the world. Almost from the start, however, "ping-pong," as the game was and is popularly called, developed on two levels: the pleasure-producing pitty-pat game, and the high powered competitive game. They are worlds apart.

Early descriptions of table tennis depict a "net" improvised by British Army officers, from books laid across the center of a long mess table, wooden "racquets" or "bats," a small cork ball, and rules made up as the sport developed. Early on, the score became established as 21 points, and the customs of serving evolved. The first celluloid ball is reputed to have been found in the United States around 1891 by a British cross-country runner named Gibbs, the ball having been manufactured as a toy. (The name of the manufacturer is not known.) Soon, a friend of Gibbs, one J. Jacques (apparently a manufacturer of some sort), registered the name "Ping-Pong," chosen, obviously, for the onomatopoetic sound of this ball as it rebounded from a briefly fashionable hollow vellum racquet then in use.) Previous to "ping-pong," Jacques' firm had marketed its version of the game as "Gossimar." There is no satisfactory explanation for this odd name.

It is difficult to credit the speed with which this parlor game swept the world, first as a novelty, later as a competitive sport. By 1904, more than a dozen different formalized rules were developed by

61

various entrepreneurs who sought to cash in on the fad. Then, for almost two decades, interest in the game nearly vanished. Only a few clubs in England, Europe, and the Far East continued competitive play. How much recreational play continued in homes can only be conjectured.

Probably the greatest impetus toward revival of the game came from Parker Brothers, of Salem, Mass. This toy manufacturing company (which was later to attain world renown from its invention of the Depression spawned board game, Monopoly), purchased the rights to the name "Ping-Pong" and formed the American Ping-Pong Association, a purely commercial undertaking, around 1925. Previous to this time, one E.C. Goode, of Putney, England, fabricated a pimpled-rubber cover for a wooden blade, thus giving birth to the first really suitable table tennis racquet, or paddle. (Leather, cloth, cork and sandpaper coverings, even stringed racquets, had all been previously tried and found wanting.) The impact of the Parker Brothers sales promotion should not be underrated. Although the pimpled-rubber blade had been available for more than 20 years, not until this company embarked on its total push for Ping-Pong did the game emerge from obscurity. This racquet was to reign supreme for thirty years.

Competitive associations were now formed with astonishing speed: the English Table Tennis Association, the American Table Tennis Association, associations in various other countries throughout the world, and in 1926, the International Table Tennis Federation. It should be noted that these associations veered away from using Ping-Pong in their names, partly because of its nursery school sound, but more practically because of its registration as a copyrighted name for the Parker line of equipment and carrying, presumably, penalties for infringement. In 1934, equipment manufacturers settled their differences, and "ping-pong" has become almost a generic term for table tennis.

Now table tennis is played, competitively and as a pleasant pastime, in almost every country all over the globe, yet the two forms of the game are still worlds apart. Good so-called "parlor players" have never striven to compete in the same leagues as national and international champions. Even rule changes (such as the formalities of the serve), have gone by unnoticed by players at the purely recreational level.

The most dramatic change in competitive table tennis appeared in the 1950's with the introduction of a different kind of table tennis racquet and its concomitant form of play. Rules of the game have

Note the angle of the racquet, or paddle, as the player imparts spin with a sharp downward move.

never specified an official racquet (as is also the case in tennis and badminton), so that enthusiasts of the sport have been totally free to experiment. In 1952, the Japanese astonished the competitive world when they introduced the skillful use of the sponge rubber racquet. The wooden blade is covered by a layer of sponge. The surface is then covered by another rubber layer, three kinds of which being currently in fashion: one in which the pimpled surface faces out, one where the pimples face in, and a peculiar sponge with spin-dampening characteristics. Some racquets even combine two characteristics by having different surfaces on each side.

The result of this new racquet was to revolutionize the game. Hard rubber surfaced bats proved ineffective against sponge. Outstanding players, gifted in the clever strokes and startling ball control of the game, now found it impossible to prolong a rally—attacking, defending, changing speeds, awaiting the chance to move in on a kill—in the face of the unpredictable but controlled spin that sponge surfaces provided. Furthermore, the customary sound of ball on paddle had disappeared, muted to the vanishing point by the sponge racquet's soft surfaces, thus making it impossible to anticipate the kind of return of the ball from the sound. And finally, the very nature (and, for the spectators, the total drama) of the game had changed. No longer were there exchanges lasting for many minutes. (One lasting an hour and 15 minutes is on record.) No more was there need for a time rule in games which threatened to run on for several hours. No more would there be the familiar pattern of the "chop" player, belly to the table, competing against the "driver," 20 to 30 feet back from the table's edge—neither player predictable as the sure winner. Now the game had changed to a half dozen quick exchanges, the ball moving too fast for spectator appreciation, and the game quickly ending. Indeed, the yen for speedy contests has resulted in an "expedite" system rule. This rule, once designed as an option to bring to a close seemingly endless rallies between evenly matched opponents, now is applied to entire games which are not finished in the incredibly short time of 15 minutes. (After this length of time, players are limited to 12 returns each in which to complete a point.)

It is difficult to refrain from taking sides—either the older game as played with hard rubber racquets or the modern competitive game as played with sponge. Now and then, exhibitions of the older style are given, and still attract an admiring audience. Also most recreational players scarcely realize that their hard rubber bats are considered hopelessly old fashioned by the top competitors, nor do they have any idea of the spins possible should they invest in good sponge racquets. Indeed, hard rubber bats are still produced and sold by the thousands, along with shoddy sponge, designed to cash in on the new market, for the new game draws the high-powered competition, and those who would emulate this sort of play. Even if it does not attract the admiring, it is, at this time, the preferred form of top-flight play.

The Game

Table tennis is the only one of the games discussed in this book where volleyed shots are not allowed. It is played by two players (singles) or four players (doubles) who stand at a table and strike a small celluloid ball back and forth across a miniature net, using small, rubber covered wooden racquets. The table measures five feet by nine and stands 2½ feet above the floor. The net is six inches high. Playing surface is usually wood, preferably painted a dark green of the matte type.

Countless games are played on tables that do not begin to meet these standards. Thousands of schools and recreation centers still make do with spray painted ¾-inch ply, measuring but four by eight feet,

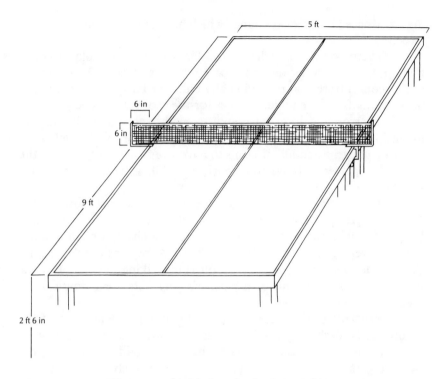

Diagram of table tennis playing surface.

placed over wooden saw horses of indeterminate height. Table tennis kits, ranging from shoddy to elegant, are purchased regularly, again in the many thousands, and may be found in locations so cramped as to give but inches of clearance for players or in spacious complexes where they are used in conjunction with other sports. Pool halls, bowling centers, racquetball clubs, regular table tennis "emporiums," college dorms, and "Y's" are among the favorites.

Many players remain at the "easy-pat" stage of play. Others move to mastery of a variety of strokes and spin-controlled shots. But the person who gets more deeply into the game finds it to be an extremely vigorous sport, demanding peak physical condition, excellent eye-hand coordination, and intense concentration. These advanced players now enter into the techniques which require meticulous finesse and the mastery of strokes that impart spin. A reliable serve and the push shot are basic, followed by the ability to block, drive, lob, and smash. These strokes are often learned with the hard-faced racquet. The change to the sponge racquet makes possible learning the so-called "loop" shots, special drop shots, and chops. Then the game turns into the swift-paced charging exchange which baffles the nonplayer with its ferocity.

There was a time when a top-flight competitive player could build a game on either defensive or offensive strategy. The defensive player concentrated on retrieving any ball sent back, often retreating many yards from the table, waiting for the more aggressive player to make an error and lose the point. Even though many players still might have a more natural aptitude and preference for this defensive type of game, the pendulum seems to have swung definitely toward the aggressive player. Attack ferociously and kill is now the standard strategy.

The dancing footwork and forceful arm and wrist moves of the skilled player give the advanced game its strenuous quality. Many hours of daily practice are required to build a champion. In doubles play, an even more frantic quality enters the game for the rules require that the doubles partners alternate turns in striking the ball. Just the necessity for keeping out of a partner's way puts great physical demands on a player.

Regardless of the level of play, table tennis is another of the racquet sports which grant instant success and fun to the beginner. Skills learned in this game bring no harm—no bad habits—to other racquet games. Indeed, the opposite is more likely to be the case because of the physical and psychological demands inherent in the game.

Equipment

The racquet

Rules of table tennis do not stipulate the size, shape, or weight of the racquet (often referred to as "bat" or "paddle"). However, with the coming of sponge rubber, the total thickness of the face cannot exceed four millimeters. The racquet face covers must also be similar in color and dark. The facings may be of rubber or wood. Typically racquets measure about 12 inches from tip to tip, the handle being about four inches in length. (There are also more abbreviated handles.) The racquet face, called a "blade," measures about eight by six inches. The blade is most commonly made from laminated wood. Shapes vary somewhat, from wedge-shaped to curved, the latter being more common. Racquet weight is from five to seven ounces.

Left: The grip shown is the one most commonly used. Right: The spread of the fingers on the racquet blade is this player's adaptation of the handshake grip.

The ball

Most table tennis balls are made of celluloid. They are hollow and must measure not more than 1½ inches in diameter. They may be no more than 39 grains in weight. When dropped from a height of one foot they should rebound to 10 inches.

The table

The standard five by nine table must be solid enough to provide the uniform bounce previously mentioned in the ball test. Usually the surface is wood, painted a dark green, with a surface that is not slick. Lines are simple, consisting of a ¾ inch white borderline around the entire table. The table is supported so that the surface is 2½ feet above the floor.

The net measures six inches in height, and is six feet long. The extra inches extend to special net supports attached to the table, which hold the net posts about six inches from the sides of the table.

Clothing

The rules specify that table tennis clothing may not be white, because of the difficulty in seeing the white ball against a white background. Also, players may not wear colors that might distract the opponent.

Most players wear dark tops, dark shorts, and the tennis shoes of their preference.

Play of the Ball

The ball is put in play by the server, who stands anywhere behind the end of the table but not beyond imaginary lines extended from the sides. The ball must be held in the flat of the palm of the non-racquet hand, tossed in the air, then struck with the racquet in such a way that it bounces first on the server's side, then rebounds to the receiver's side across the net. After bouncing on the receiver's side, it is then rallied back and forth until an error is made or until an outstanding shot makes it impossible for a return. Errors consist of balls struck on a second bounce, volleyed, hit into the net, or hit so that they fail to strike the table surface across the net.

Each player holds the serve for five successive points. Either the server or the receiver may score points. Game score is 21.

Fundamentals

The grip

Two types of grip are currently in vogue, and both will be described. The first and oldest grip is the traditional handshake grip, in which the blade is perpendicular to the floor and the hand grasps the handle of the racquet. However, unlike the grip used in all other racquet sports, the forefinger is not wrapped around the handle. Instead, it extends along the bottom of the blade, not protruding onto the face of the blade itself. The thumb also is braced against the blade, rather than against the index finger, and should not obtrude upon the playing surface of the blade. This grip suffices for both forehand and

*A legal serve requires that the ball be tossed from the palm of the free
hand, then struck before the bounce.*

backhand; the forehand side being that with the thumb, the backhand
that with the index finger.

The second type of grip (one mastered first by the Chinese and
now the preferred grip in the Orient), is the pen-holder grip. Although
there are several variations in the placement of the three supporting
fingers, the racquet handle is placed so that it nestles between the
thumb and index fingers which wrap around and meet at the base of
the blade. The ball is played off this blade face both for backhand and
forehand.

The handshake grip allows for greater reach and heavier
backhand stroking. The pen-holder demands exceedingly fast footwork but saves time in that only one face of the racquet is used. A
great debate still rages, extolling the virtues of each grip. Right now
the inverted sponge seems to have influenced the argument in favor of
the handshake grip.

The player imparts power with the whole body and spin from the blade angle.

Stance

The "get-ready" position appears fundamental to advanced table tennis play. The player stands a few feet back from the mid-point of the table, in a slight crouch, knees bent. One foot may be slightly forward. When time permits, the body pivots sideways to the ball—left side forward on the forehand, right for the backhand. (These instructions are, of course, for the right-handed player.)

Stroking

Power is directed to the ball not only from arm swing but from the legs, waist, and body. The left arm supplies balance, and is generally carried in a bent position, close to the body. The strokes are made with the right arm bent at the elbow, rather than out from the body and fully extended. The ball is best met well in front of the body. Only in desperation is it contacted at the side.

The block is a defensive shot.

Footwork

Steps are usually small and dancing. In general, the first step is taken with the foot away from the stroke. That is to say, in moving to the right, the left foot crosses over first as a pivot is made on the right foot. The player tries to return to the basic get-ready position after each stroke.

Spin

Almost every table tennis stroke carries spin to the ball. This is determined by the angle of the blade face when it contacts the ball and on its follow-through. Blade angles may be open (facing toward the ceiling), or closed (facing toward the table). Only occasionally are they neutral (neither open nor closed).

Strokes

The push

Basic to beginning table tennis is the push. As the name implies,

This page and opposite: The classic forehand drive.

it is a short move, taken backhand or forehand, and intended chiefly to return the ball. The racquet face is slightly open. The brief follow-through toward the table top imparts a slight back spin to the ball.

The chop

In the chop, the ball is more briskly stroked than in the push. The blade is brought down sharply, in a chopping motion, and the ball receives decisive back spin.

The block

Used mostly as a defensive stroke, the block meets the ball on the rise. The racquet angle is designed to counteract the opponent's spin: open against chops, closed against top spin. There is little back swing and very controlled follow-through.

The lob

Another defensive stroke, the lob is used when an opponent's shot forces a player back from the table. The ball is met as it drops, and is contacted as low as possible. The arm is brought well back for a full stroke, the blade comes under the ball, and is brought up and over, giving top spin. The ball is directed upwards as high as possible.

Drives

Current drives show a great amount of sophistication in their delivery. Low, flat drives, directed to all parts of the playing surface, have long been basic to the game. With the arrival of the sponge covered blade, the loop drive has made its appearance (see the photo on page 60). In this stroke, the racquet meets the ball with a closed face. Follow-through is high, around the head. Extreme top spin is applied by snapping the wrist and rolling the forearm on contact. The blade face is parallel to the table at the conclusion of the stroke.

Side spins may also be imparted to the ball by advanced players. In general, side spin results from a sweeping motion on a drive and the follow-through is taken with an open-blade face.

Smashes and kills

Here the ball is met high, in front of the body, at the top of the bounce, and straight on. Power is the key, for the smash or kill is meant to put away a high, weak shot set up inadvertently by the opponent.

Drop shots

Effective when an opponent has been forced back from the table, the drop shot requires a delicate touch and deceptive moves. The defending opponent should be fooled into thinking that the stroke is going to be another power stroke. The body and racquet should be over the ball, the racquet high. As the ball bounces, it is touched gently just as it rises above net level, and is stroked with but a small movement of the racquet. Open or closed face is determined by the spin the opponent has put on the ball.

Only practice can show an aspiring player how to develop a competitive game. With each refinement of attack comes an equally effective refinement on defense. This game of speed and spin and exciting angles has probably not yet reached its developmental peak. The student of table tennis, therefore, can best learn more about the game by playing it.

Courtesies

There appears to be a considerable amount of "psyching" between opponents in table tennis matches. Also, it is not unusual for players to address the referee in cases where rulings are made that might be considered controversial. Such galleries as there might be in table tennis matches do not maintain traditional silences during rallies. However, it would be inaccurate to assume that table tennis players are ill-mannered toward each other. As in all good competition, good sporting behavior, albeit more casual than in other racquet sports, is the general rule.

Rules

Service may be decided by the toss of a coin. More informally, one player holds both hands below the table, grasping a table tennis ball in one of them. The opponent guesses the hand. The winner of the guess may choose either to serve or receive.

In the serve, the rules describe how the free hand holding the ball must be in such a position that spin cannot be imparted to the ball by a twist of the fingers. The ball rests in the hand, and is definitely tossed into the air, not dropped, in performing the legal serve. There is a common misapprehension that the ball must strike shallow enough on the receiver's side so that a second bounce, were it allowed, would occur on the table. It is hard to say where this idea got its start, but it may be ascribed, perhaps, to a rule adapted for the benefit of beginning players. Beginners are also allowed to hold the ball in any way possible to get it into play—the toss from the open palm requiring far more coordination than holding the ball in the fingers. Once the player progresses beyond the beginning stages, however, these nursery forms of play should be abandoned in favor of the rules of the game.

A "let" occurs on serve if the ball touches the net on its way to the opponent's court, but is otherwise legal. A let is played over. The rules also describe other situations which might call for a let or replay.

Game score is 21 points, except when a game is tied at 20-all. In this case the winner must be two points ahead. The serve changes hands after every serve until this game point is played.

Matches are generally three out of five games.

A player is never allowed to touch the net.

The "expedite system" may be applied to a game which is unfinished after 15 minutes of play. In this case the server must win the point within 12 strokes after the serve.

Special rules regarding serving order, placement of serve, and return of the ball are designed for doubles play. Rules are available, often free, at sporting goods stores and table tennis centers. They are also printed in various books on table tennis.

Professional Play

Although players in some European countries (such as Sweden and Germany) are often subsidized so that they can make good livings in table tennis, there is very little opportunity for this kind of life style in the United States. Top players can receive pay for endorsing equipment. Sometimes tournaments carry prize money. Coaching and managing table tennis centers can be profitable businesses. And demonstration sessions, using both hard rubber racquets and the sponge rubber, bring in good retainers. But, for the most part, the outstanding table tennis competitor must earn a living in some endeavor other than the sport.

Furthermore, even with all the continued interest in the game, it is unlikely that table tennis will take over as a true spectator sport: the kind of sport that pays its professionals. For a time, it looked as though there might be a growing, paying audience. But the kind of play engendered by the sponge rubber racquet appears to have brought an end to that idea.

Organizations

The United States Table Tennis Association
12 Lake Ave
Merrick NY 11566
(Publishes *Table Tennis Topics*, monthly, ed. Tim Boggins)

Chapter 5

Racquets

History

Racquets, like court tennis, is a game of such antiquity that its beginnings are lost in history. Robert W. Henderson, in his book *Ball, Bat and Bishop*, reiterates the thesis (one generally in favor among anthropologists), that all forms of tennis and other racquet sports have a common ancestry in Egyptian and Arabic games, tracing a tenuous but credible thread back to 15 centuries before the birth of Christ. However, he also states that the earliest mention of the game of racquets in modern history is in a poem written by the Scotsman, William Dunbar, somewhere around the year 1500. The poem speaks of racquet players and tennis players ("sa mony rakketis, sa mony ket-che-pillaris"), evidence, perhaps, that tennis and racquets developed side by side. Even in the present day, the annual schedule for racquets contests in North America coincides with that of the court tennis schedule and is published and publicized in the same announcements.

Although racquets in some form is believed to have been played in early court tennis enclosures during the 16th century, the game as now recognized probably had its origin in Debtor's Prison, England, at a date not precisely known. Charles Dickens describes a one-walled racquets game popular among prison inmates who, not being hardened criminals, were granted free time during which they indulged themselves with games of handball. Soon wooden paddles were being whittled to afford some sort of protection against the hard ball used. It is hypothesized that when debtors returned to society, they brought the game with them. Predictably, wealthy aristocrats found the game

78

Few squash players have ever seen the immense racquets court from which their game, properly called "squash racquets," is descended. This view is from the spectator's gallery of the Boston Tennis and Racquet Club court (one of nine courts remaining in North America).

both interesting and fashionable to play. But not until 1822, when students of Harrow School began competing in racquets contests against other schools, could it be said that the game had truly arrived.

Weather drove the game indoors. Rules were altered, at last allowing players to utilize all four walls in play. Elaborate courts were built, appearing in England, Canada, and the United States. By the end of the 19th century, racquets was the game of prestige among the aristocracy and the wealthy, reaching its peak just before World War I.

Its decline in the 1920's was swift, the reasons only partially understood. The expense of building and maintaining the large, over-sized concrete racquets courts surely contributed much to its slide from popularity. Players were finding satisfaction in squash racquets, a more circumscribed form of the game requiring a comparatively modest outlay of money for playing facilities — squash racquets courts needing approximately half the room of racquets courts. In any event, and for whatever reason, the game almost died out. Now there remain but nine clubs in the North American Racquets Association. These clubs are located in Detroit and Chicago (each have two clubs); Boston, Philadelphia, Tuxedo Park, N.Y., New York, and Montreal.

In this exclusive circle, the game still maintains its popularity. Matches are played internationally against the few remaining clubs in Great Britain, and the enthusiasm among the players of the sport is boundless. Yet is is unlikely that any new racquets courts will ever be constructed. Probably the game will continue to be played only so long as the present courts are maintained.

The Game

Racquets is a game of strength, coordination, and agility, requiring great bursts of effort and extremely quick reaction time, played at its best in an environment that presents elements of real danger to the contestants. A hard, small ball is struck with a long, stringed racquet (called a "racquets bat" — "racquets racquet" being rather de trop), and rebounds from concrete walls and floor during the course of play. The game has an explosive quality. The large, concrete enclosure of the court fills with the sound like the crack of a small-bore rifle as the rock-like ball ricochets about the arena, reaching speeds estimated up to 200 miles per hour.

Racquets is played by two or four players (singles or doubles) who contest in an immense court, the measurements now standardized at 30 by 60 feet, giving a surface area of 1800 square feet — immense as compared with the 592 square feet of American squash racquets, 672 square feet for British squash racquets, and the 800 square feet of racquetball. (At one time, before court size was standardized, courts measuring 40 by 80 feet were not uncommon.) Front and side walls extend upwards to 30 feet, and the back wall, which houses a viewing gallery above, to 15 feet. (The highest wall-playing surface in squash racquets is 22 feet, depending upon the shape of the room; of racquetball, 20 feet.) The entire enclosure is slick concrete, the harder the better, treated with a patented surfacing to promote fast rebound and

Differences in equipment used in racquets and squash racquets are easily seen in this comparison photo. The racquets bat and ball are at the top.

unpredictable spin. Both floor and walls are dark in color, almost black. The ball is white. Lines on the court mark service boxes and service areas (see diagram). Entrance to the court is through a door at the rear wall, cut flush with the concrete.

A ball is played against the walls using a long-handled stringed racquet. The ceiling is out-of-bounds, as is a small strip on the lower front wall: a 27 inch board covered with heavy padding. Called the "tell-tale," its distinctive sound reports an illegal hit should a ball strike it. The serving side may win a point by serving an "ace" (a shot that cannot be played on), winning a rally, or profiting by the receiving side's error. The receiving side may earn the right to serve, although with no point awarded, by winning a rally or profiting from the serving side's error. The first side to score 15 points wins the game. A match is the best three out of five games.

Singles and doubles games are official forms of racquets competition, recognized in the United States, Canada, and abroad. Amateur and open championships are annual events and customarily draw entrants from all of the active clubs.

Rules are discussed in more detail at the end of the chapter.

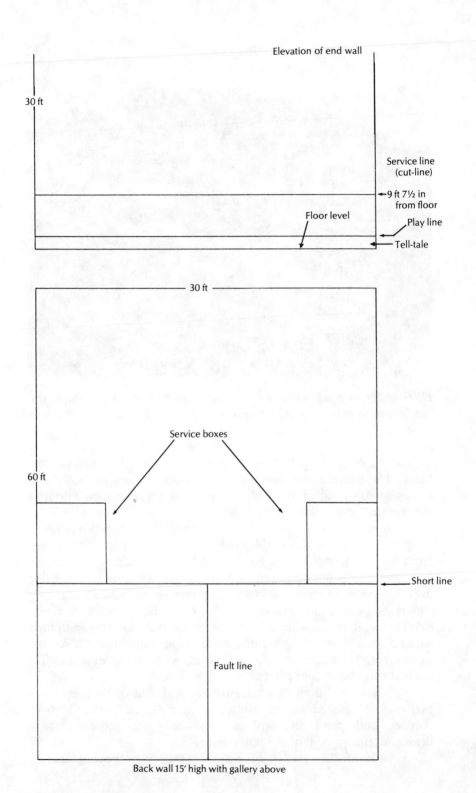

Elevation of end wall

30 ft

Service line
(cut-line)

9 ft 7½ in
from floor

Play line

Floor level

Tell-tale

30 ft

Service boxes

60 ft

Short line

Fault line

Back wall 15' high with gallery above

Equipment

The racquet

The modern racquets bat is made of ash, and is approximately 30 inches long. The head is nearly circular, seven to eight inches in diameter, and lightly strung with gut. It weighs about nine ounces. The bat is subject to great stress, often colliding with the floor or walls in the heat of play. A bat may last as little as a week or, with luck, as long as a season. The Grays racquet, made in England, is the only racquet available.

The ball

Racquets balls are one inch in diameter and weigh an ounce. They are comprised of a hard plastic sphere, bound with twine, and covered with a sticky backed cotton tape. It is customary to have a number of balls available for play, even several dozen, to keep the game moving. Balls out of play are pushed into small receptacles located in floor wells at either end of the tell-tale. Racquets balls are generally the property of the club and furnished for play.

Clothing

Official rules specify that the player's attire must be white. Tennis shoes are worn, the style a matter of individual preference.

Play of the Ball

In singles, the ball is put in play by the server, called "hand-in," who may elect to start the game from either of the service boxes. The hand-in must have one foot within the service box as the serve is delivered. The ball is tossed into the air, then struck to the forward wall where it must hit above the "cut-line" (the line 9 feet 7½ inches from the floor) and rebound into the court beyond the short-line in the service area opposite the service box from which the ball is delivered. The receiver, called "hand-out," may return the ball to any wall,

Opposite: Back wall (top) and court diagram for racquets (front wall would be at the bottom).

The grip is the same for all strokes; all hits should impart spin to the ball.

provided that at some point the ball reaches the front wall before touching the floor. The players alternate in making returns until one player fails to make a good return.

The volley, the half-volley, "boasted" hits, and the kill are important strokes in this game, but the most important one is the serve. Here the experienced player can take control of the game by imparting spin on the ball with a heavily cut stroke, causing the ball to rebound from front to side wall and reach the opponent so that it cannot be easily returned.

Good play is concentrated mostly on low, hard hit shots. A particularly effective hit is a "drop," a ball struck so that it just reaches the front wall, then drops close to it. In the "half-volley" the ball is struck just as it contacts the floor and before it has time to rise. (It can be seen that this stroke accounts for much of the heavy attrition on the racquets bats.) The "boasted" stroke is one in which the ball is struck into any of the other walls before it reaches the front wall. The "volley" is a ball struck before the bounce. The "kill" is, as the name implies, a stroke that when properly done cannot be defended against.

Racquets is not a game that grants easy success, although the newcomer can soon enjoy a hit by dint of great concentration and repeated self-admonitions. ("Watch the ball." "Remember the racquet is 30 inches long.") Indeed, it is not so much the difference in timing which baffles, for example, the tennis player who decides to try the game, as that great, long lightweight bat with its tiny, seven-inch racquet face, which repeatedly causes over-reaching, and a distressing ricochet from the wooden throat of the bat. Also, early experiences with the game are generally free from the wild speed of the flying ball, typical of the game as played by experts, which gives the sport its reputation of danger. Experienced players initiate the beginner into the intricacies of racquets rather carefully.

The most successful newcomers to the game reach it through experience in squash racquets, and are often caught up by the sport, exulting in the freedom of the larger court and the excitement of playing the small, hard ball. Most racquets clubs also house squash racquets courts. Unfortunately for the future development of the game of racquets, the opposite is not true.

Fundamentals

Forehand

The racquet is held in a traditional handshake grip, well down on the bat handle, with the stringed face slightly open (i.e., turned slightly clockwise) although nearly vertical to the floor. The hand is well spread along the grip.

In the forehand stroke, the right-handed player addresses the ball with the left side of the body turned toward the target, weight well back on the right foot, knees bents, both feet on the floor, right arm back and wrist cocked. The stroke is executed with a moderate arm sweep, the right shoulder drops, the wrist snaps into an extended position as the strings hit the ball. The weight shifts to the left foot, the follow-through is toward the player's left rather than toward the target. On impact, the ball is just about opposite the player's left toe.

Because of the dangers inherent in flailing about with a 30-inch bat in a crowded playing area, the stroke, while extremely powerful, is curiously circumscribed. The long bat also necessitates intense concentration on the ball. Even experienced players make occasional "wood shots," resulting in unpredictable and sometimes dangerous flights of the ball.

Backhand

Most players do not shift the grip for this stroke. Indeed, the pace of a well-played game seldom gives time for a grip change. As the ball approaches, the player's right side is now toward it, the arm with the wrist cocked back across the body, and the weight on the left foot.

In executing the stroke, the player makes the weight transfer by stepping toward the ball with the right foot. On impact, the ball is met farther toward the target than in the forehand, and the follow-through is short.

The volley

Both the volley and the half-volley are short, crisp strokes in which the bat blocks the ball. There is very little back swing or follow-through. In the half-volley, the ball is taken just after it begins its rebound from the floor. The stringed racquet face is open, causing the ball to glance off at an angle. Volleys are more often directed to side and back walls than to the front wall, although the use of any stroke depends on the particular instant in the game and the expertise of the player.

The serve

Advanced players use both forehand and backhand strokes in delivering the serve. A right-handed player, when delivering a forehand serve from the service box on the right side, often finds that facing the wall to the right cuts off a split second in repositioning for the return. Therefore, many players deliver from the right service box with a backhand stroke and from the left service box with a forehand.

The movement of the bat may be underhand, parallel, or overhand. Usually it is underhand or parallel, for the ball must strike first above the cut-line, more than nine feet from the court surface, in order to be legal.

The most effective strokes in racquets, service included, are delivered with "cut." The open-faced positioning of the racquet, combined with a stroke that moves under the ball, imparts spin. Variations in spin make the ball ricochet from the walls as cushion shots do in billiards, thus the game among advanced players develops astonishing variations both in design and pace.

Opposite: The forehand sequence.

The ready position for forehand serve.

Rules

Some of the rules have been touched upon in the section under "Play of the Ball." The discussion following is based on *"The Laws of Racquets"* as printed in the rules book of the Boston Tennis and Racquets Club.

Choice of serve is decided by spin of the racquet. The server has but one chance to make a good serve (a change from the rules of

Opposite: The backhand sequence.

Even in so large a court, players are subject to a degree of danger from the hard ball and the long bats. The thin diagonal blur above the player on the right is the ball in flight.

several years ago when, under certain conditions, a second serve was allowed.)

Errors in play include failing to strike the ball before the second bounce on the court, hitting the ball out-of-bounds or into the tell-tale, allowing the ball to touch the clothing of the player who last struck it, and impeding the opportunity of the opponent to make a fair play. Provisions are made for declaring a replay, called "let," in cases such as reasonable fear of injury in making a hit, or a ball breaking during play (neither of these occurences being unusual).

Racquets gives the hand-out the option of volleying the serve (i.e., striking the ball before it touches the court). A serve so volleyed is considered "good" no matter where the hand-out contacts the ball.

In scoring, although the official game consists of 15 points, should the game be tied at 13-all, the first to reach 13 has the option of adding five more or three more points to the game, called "setting," or allowing the regular score to stand. At 14-all, the same option is available to set the game at three.

Doubles rules deal for the most part with the service and receiving order. The service rule provides for each member of the doubles team to serve during the team's hand-in. Except for the first hand-in of each game, each player serves until the point or "stroke" is lost. Because only the hand-in side scores points, it is considered too great an advantage to give the serving team two turns at the start of the game. (Indeed, the *Encyclopaedia Britannica* cites a match played in 1897 at the Queen's Club in England when W.L. Foster served a series of 36 aces in a row, finally losing hand-in during the third game. This record clearly demonstrates the importance of a skillful serve.

Rules also provide for the receivers or hand-out players to establish a set order at the start of each game so that the reception of the served ball alternates between them.

The player in possession of the serve at the end of a game begins the next game as server.

Professional Play

It is regrettable that racquets, both amateur and professional, is limited in its player and spectator participation. Professionalism refers simply to small purses in few contests, and to salaried player-coaches at clubs. As previously stated, the future of racquets appears to be linked to the handful of courts currently in use.

Organizations

North American Racquets Association
   William Surtees, President
   Racquet and Tennis Club
   370 Park Ave
   New York NY 10022

Tennis and Rackets Association
   York House
   37 Queen Square
   London, W.C. 1, England

Chapter 6

Squash Racquets

History

There should be no problem in tracing the history of squash racquets (more familiarly known as "squash") for it is the direct descendent of racquets (see Chapter 5). However, even this game presents some interesting detours when trying to establish its beginnings and trace its growth. There is little doubt that squash appeared first at Harrow School in England, presumably as a warmup game when students were idling away their time, awaiting their turns at the racquets court. The date is not definitely known—estimates from 1850 to 1880 are mentioned in the literature—although the earlier date seems more reasonable. Also, the game evolved in various ways in different locales.

For many years no standards were established for the squash balls other than that they be India Rubber and "squashy" (as compared with those used in racquets). Somehow the racquet lost two to three inches in length. And the only standards for courts were that they be considerably smaller than racquets courts. Even the scoring went its own particular way. Games played in England and the British Empire went to nine points with only the serving side scoring points. In the United States, either the server or the receiver could score points and the game went to 15. These differences in court size, ball specifications, and scoring persist to the present.

Squash racquets reached the United States by way of Montreal, Canada, in 1882. It was played in St. Paul's School, New Hampshire, but soon underwent a further change when a tennis ball and a kind of

The squash racquets court viewed from the spectators' gallery shows it to be a much smaller version of the racquets court.

tennis racquet were substituted for the squash equipment. For a while, "squash tennis" (as the game was called) achieved tremendous popularity, threatening to crowd out the older game. But the fad wore itself out, and squash tennis is seldom played now.

The first attempts to codify rules of the squash racquets game were made around 1922, in England, when the Tennis and Rackets Association formed a subcommittee to investigate the lack of uniformity in the various squash games. Shortly after, in 1923, the newly formed United States Squash Racquets Association standardized the game for its part of the world, arriving at dimensions of 18½ by 32 feet for the singles court and keeping the harder and livelier American ball. Four years later, in 1928, for reasons never clearly stated, the English court was standardized at 21 feet by 32 feet. At the same time the English association kept the squashier ball which had never gained favor in America. The nonstandardization of the squash courts and balls compounded the problems in the game, even to this day. Ironically, only in doubles is there presently no problem with standardization.

The irony lies in the fact that the singles game is the more popular form of competition and that doubles came into fashion only in the United States. A larger court, measuring 25 by 45 feet, was designed for a proper doubles game, and the livelier ball presented no problem for the doubles game. Nowadays it is played in international competition. Yet there are only some 300 doubles courts in the world, most of which are in the United States, whereas the singles courts number in the thousands and are, of course, worldwide.

Further differences appear in court markings (the English court using squares to delineate the service boxes; the American, pie-shaped enclosures), in out-of-bounds lines (the tell-tale being two inches lower in the United States and the back wall line six inches higher), and in the scoring, as previously mentioned. Markings and out-of-bounds lines influence the game to some extent, especially at high-level play, but scoring methods impart their own particular flavor to a game.

Partly in an attempt to standardize squash rules, the International Squash Rackets Federation held its inaugural meeting in London early in 1967, with Great Britain, Australia, India, New Zealand, Pakistan, South Africa, and the United Arab Republic as founding members. After an indeterminate length of time spent in puzzling over working around the differences between ISRF rules and those of the North American game, the United States and Canada were allowed to join as founding members—a technicality which makes considerable difference in voting power. The Federation now

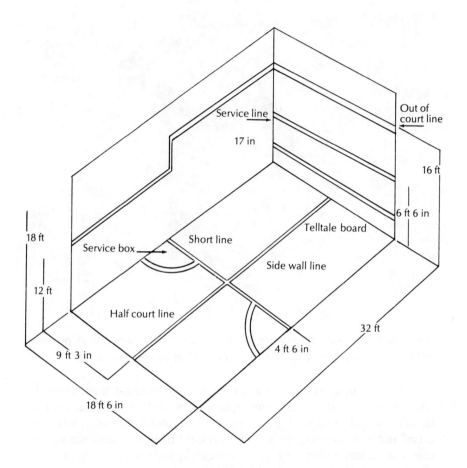

Service line

Out of court line

17 in

16 ft

6 ft 6 in

18 ft

Service box

Short line

Telltale board

12 ft

Side wall line

Half court line

32 ft

9 ft 3 in

4 ft 6 in

18 ft 6 in

Diagram of squash court

works from the SRA offices in London, and its annual international championships are considered to be the unofficial world's championship matches.

The Women's Squash Rackets Association was formed in England in 1934, and a similar organization (using, once more, the American preference for the spelling, "racquets") in America shortly after. Professional and college associations also exist. In the face of all these organizations, the newcomer to squash might well be astounded by the disparate rules still obtaining throughout the world, particularly if the player is experienced in tennis or badminton or any of the other racquet sports which have been standardized for decades.

The player in the foreground waits at the "T" where the two main court lines cross, while her opponent prepares to return the ball.

Of course, many if not all of these interesting differences in what is, presumably, the same sport, may still be credited to the leisurely world in which the game developed. Now, however, with jet travel and satellite communication, it is hard to justify the anomaly of their continuance. But they seem to be pretty well dug in on both sides of the Atlantic, remaining as both irritant and spice in one of the world's most popular racquet sports.

The Game

Squash racquets is a game of fast action, requiring great strength, conditioning, speed, swift reaction time, and eye-hand coordination. In its most popular form, two contestants take turns striking a small, spongy ball against the walls of an indoor court, using long-handled stringed racquets.

Court dimensions differ slightly according to the country in which the game is played. Markings on the floor, side walls, back wall, and front wall are simple, delineating service boxes, service areas, and boundaries for play (see diagram). Like racquets, squash has a "tell-tale" at the front wall: a strip of sheet metal running along the bottom. Shots hitting the tell-tale are out of play. Also, as in racquets, the ceiling is out-of-bounds. Entrance to the court is from a small door set flush in the back wall, above which is a viewing gallery. Or the door may be let into the side wall near the back, particularly if the court has been constructed with a glass backwall, glass doors being very expensive.

Basic strokes in squash include the serve, backhand, forehand, and volley. Lobs and drop shots are also used by advanced players.

Equipment

The racquet

Rules of the game specify that the overall length of a squash racquet shall not exceed 27 inches. The head is 8½ inches long by 7¼ inches wide. Although recently metal shafts have been used, squash racquets are usually made of wood. All-metal racquets are considered to be too dangerous.

The ball

The diameter of the ball is just over 1½ inches. It is rubber and hollow. The English ball is very spongy as compared with the American ball and is considered unsuitable for doubles. There is no real agreement between nations on the suitability or unsuitability of the singles ball. While the former "hardball" used in American play is still technically "official," all major tournaments, all National Championships (singles), and college and professional play is with the so-called "70+" type of ball, and the term "North American Green" covers both. These balls are made by Merco of Australia and distributed by West Company.

Clothing

In 1967, the ISRF adopted the SRA rule making it obligatory for players to wear white clothing, but current rulings allow pastel colors for USSRA play, so long as they are solid colors. Players usually wear shorts and lightweight tops. Tennis shoes are a matter of individual preference.

The server (foreground) needs but one foot in the service box when delivering a legal serve.

Play of the Ball

The ball is put in play by the server who stands with at least one foot in the service box. The ball is tossed in the air, or bounced, then hit to the front wall where it must strike above the service line and rebound to the service court opposite the service box from which it was delivered. (The ball may even be bounced off the side wall, or whatever, so long as once struck by the racquet it goes directly to the front wall.) The player returning the ball may direct it to any wall, so long as at some time the ball reaches the front wall before touching the floor. The players alternate in making returns until one player fails to make a good return.

The advanced squash player makes use of caroms in game strategy. Because the ball need not be returned directly to the front wall, but only must make a legal touch thereon before rebounding to the floor, innumerable angles are available to the flight of the ball. For example, in the "reverse corner" the ball travels low to the side wall, striking close to the front wall, caroms but a few feet to the front wall, then rebounds to the floor still close to the front wall: a very difficult shot to return. In a "boasted" shot the ball caroms from the far back-court side wall on a long, low diagonal almost the length of the court to the front wall close to the other side wall, thence quickly and very low to the side wall from which it dribbles to the floor: a sure winner.

Advanced players are skillful in their striving for court position and domination. A fine singles game is like a duel, where each player tries to out-think and out-maneuver the other. But basic to squash, as to all racquet games, is intense concentration on the ball and the game.

Unique to squash racquets, as well as racquets and racquetball, is the fact that a player can work out alone, designing and perfecting strokes. Because this form of practice is twice as fast, so to speak, as when an opponent is present, solo play is invaluable in developing timing and a sense of court position.

Newcomers to squash are soon delighted with their ability to keep the ball in play, particularly when competing at their own level or against players who make the game easy for them. Soon they discover the need for sharpening techniques, and game strategy enters into play. The current boom in squash and racquetball appears to be promoting tremendous interest in both sports, players at all levels (except, perhaps, for those who specialize in one or the other game) moving readily from one to the other.

Fundamentals

Forehand

The racquet is held in a traditional handshake grip, close to the butt of the handle, fingers well spread, the stringed face in a slightly closed position (i.e., rotated counter clockwise). The right-handed player addresses the ball with the left side toward the target, feet apart and parallel, knees well bent, weight back on the right foot. The arm is brought back with the elbow bent and the wrist well cocked.

In executing the stroke, the player steps onto the left foot. Simultaneously the hand and arm move and, with a strong wrist action, the racquet head is brought around to make contact with the ball. The follow-through is up and toward the target. The stroke is concise, rather than sweeping; the movement comparable to snapping a whip. Impact should come just about opposite the left foot, or a bit farther toward the target.

The player in the foreground may be unintentionally obstructing his opponent from a fair chance at the ball. If so, the point is replayed.

The mirror image of these directions describes the stroke for the left-handed player.

Backhand

Because of the quickness of the game, there is no time to change the grip in making the backhand stroke, so for most players it is the same grip as that used in the forehand. In addressing the ball, the right side is well turned, almost so that the back of the player is toward the target, weight is back on the left foot, and knees are bent. The elbow is bent, the wrist well cocked, and the racquet back.

On execution the player steps across and toward the ball, the racquet head is snapped into contact with strong wrist action, the follow-through is as complete as safety will allow. Impact is well in front of the right foot.

As in the game of racquets and racquetball, many returns do not use the full strokes of forehand and backhand. In the volley, the racquet reaches the ball before it bounces from the floor, and is a short, crisp stroke with shortened backswing and is often good for quick, offensive placements. The drop shot is mostly used on offense.

Forehand sequence; note the open racquet face on the follow-through. The stroke has imparted spin to the ball.

Opposite and above: The backhand sequence.

The ball is hit so that it barely rebounds to the floor, preferably low to the court. Skillful deception, achieved by winding up as if to make a power stroke, then cutting down on impact and follow-through, contributes to making success in using the drop shot as a winning play. Cross court drives, hit hard and deep, draw the opponent out of position, forcing a weak return. The kill, often a smash, is a consistent point maker when directed low to the corners, barely missing the tell-tale.

Excellent and detailed analysis of these techniques, as well as game strategy, may be found in *The Book of Squash*, by Peter Wood (Little, Brown & Company, Boston 1972).

Courtesies

For the most part, squash is a courteous game. The dangers inherent in moving about the confined space, swinging a 27-inch racquet at a wildly ricocheting ball, allow no physically indiscriminate action. Also, the tradition of sporting behavior is still strong. Ploys are used occasionally by some players to distract an opponent — to break the intense concentration. Customarily these are masked by courtesy: inappropriate compliments, unwonted self-deprecation, minuscule timing delays in delivering the serve — and are subtly dealt out. Noise and obstreperous behavior are not the rule on the squash court.

Rules

Squash racquets rules are simple and easy to understand. The USSRA has but 15 rules for singles in the handbook, four of which concern attire and equipment, the ball, the court, and the referee.

The serving rules stipulate that the serve is decided by the spin of the racquet. At the start of each game and each time there is a new server, the ball is served from whichever service box the server selects. It then alternates until the serve is lost or the game ends. The server has two chances to make a winning serve. In singles the person serving at

Opposite: The serving sequence.

the end of one game starts the serve for the next game. In doubles the winner of the game must serve the first point of the next game. At 17-all (a score possible when a game is "set") the winner of the final point of the game may or may not be the one serving the final point.

Either player (either team) may score points, under the United States rules. The receiver who wins a rally also wins the right to serve. Game score is 15. (In England, only the server scores points; the receiver who wins a rally earns the right to serve. Game score is 9.)

Should the score be tied at 13-all, the player first reaching 13 has the option of extending the game to 16 or 18, called "set to three" or "set to five." At 14-all, provided the score has not been at 13-all, there is a similar option to set to three, making the game 17 points.

A match is the best three out of five games.

Because of the difference in scoring, English games often go on for somewhat longer periods of time than do those played under American rules, especially with the "70 + " ball.

The most difficult problem in squash, as well as the hardest rule to interpret and enforce, is to keep out of the opponent's way. The intent of the rule and the game is to give the opponent a fair view of the ball, a fair chance to play on it, and a free access for the flight of the shot. Other rules describe illegal hits, and provisions for replays, called "lets."

Professional Play

For the most part, squash racquets competition is for the amateur. The United States has three general classifications of skill levels, as well as several age groupings. The official yearbook of the USSRA is filled with information regarding tournament play, amateur, open, and professional. But, for the most part, professional play means play in which teaching pros augment their incomes through prize money.

In promoting the sport there is a certain amount of television coverage from time to time, and newspapers often carry notices of tournaments and their results. But the nature of the game allows very little room for a gallery, therefore small chance for its development as a spectator sport. Although tournaments and exhibitions for top professionals have been increasing in number and size of purse, squash is essentially a competitor's game and only incidentally one for professionals and the viewing public.

Organizations

United States Squash Racquets Association
  211 Ford Rd
  Bala Cynwyd PA 19004
  Darwin P. Kingsley III, president

United States Women's Squash Racquets Association
  533 Kenmore Rd
  Merion Station PA 19066
  c/o Judy Michel

International Squash Rackets Federation
  4M Artillery Mansions
  Victoria St
  London, S.W. 1, England

Chapter 7

Racquetball

History

Racquetball goes back only as far as the 1950's but has its origins in a somewhat older game—paddleball (see Chapter 10).

Paddleball first emerged as a formal sport in 1930 at the University of Michigan when Earl Riskey, an instructor in physical education and intramurals, adapted the backboard practice of tennis players to create this new game. Since tennis backboard practice was taken on handball courts, Riskey quite naturally used handball rules as the basis of the paddleball rules. By giving the players a striking implement in the form of a small wooden paddle, he kept some of the leverage and power of the tennis racquet while scaling down the game to the restricted area of a handball court. The paddle also introduced a stroke not used in handball, namely the backhand.

Why did Riskey select a paddle for the striking implement rather than a stringed racquet? After all, he was at that time already familiar with the game of tennis. In his book, *Beginning Paddleball*, coauthored with Andrew J. Kozar and Rodney J. Grambeau (Wadsworth, Belmont, Calif., 1967), Riskey gives an answer. He states that he was an avid *paddle tennis* player and conducted his early experiments on his new game with a slightly cut-down paddle tennis paddle. (It should be noted that the game Riskey enjoyed is not to be confused with "paddle"—more formally known as platform—tennis. These games are discussed in Chapter 3.)

It is interesting to make the conjecture that had he used a cut-down tennis racquet, racquetball may have arrived a generation earlier

108

Top: The racquetball racquet evolved from the paddleball paddle. Bottom: The racquets suggest some of the relationship between tennis and racquetball.

as a formal sport. In any case, the game of racquetball owes much to Earl Riskey's inspiration in adapting the ancient game of handball to his new sport, paddleball.

Riskey's new game grew rapidly as an exciting form of handball. In 1952 the National Paddleball Association was formed with Earl Riskey as its first president. The first national tournament was held in 1961. The National Paddleball Committee was formalized at Michigan State University, East Lansing, in 1966.

By this time the game had evolved from a relatively simple form allowing the ball to rebound from a single backboard, through a three-walled version, into its most demanding form: a complex scramble on an indoor court with the ball ricocheting from front wall, back wall, sides and ceiling. The ball and bat had been standardized. Rules were formulated. Leagues abounded throughout the United States and Canada.

The most usual play had two opponents (singles) or two pairs of opponents (doubles). There was even a game for three known as cutthroat, which provided an excellent workout although it was not used in official competition. But still in the rules, for reasons never stated in the rulebook or in the literature of sports history, stringed racquets were expressly forbidden.

One theory has recently been advanced which seems reasonable: that the wooden tennis racquets in their cut-down form were too heavy for easy use. With the advances in technology which made possible the production of lightweight metal frames capable of withstanding tight stringing, there was no disputing that the time for racquetball had arrived. This timing seems born out by the fact that there is no record of racquetball having been played before the 1950's, and it was during the fifties that the great breakthrough came in developing metal racquets.

The International Racquetball Association was formed in 1968; it was followed by the United States Racquetball Association (for amateur play) and the National Racquetball Club (for professional play) in late 1973. Racquetball had taken the four-walled handball/paddleball courts by storm. The IRS has since disbanded and the USRA and NRC now have the responsibility for the development of rules and tournament play. (Addresses are given at the close of this chapter.)

The rules of paddleball and racquetball are nearly identical. Players in either sport can make the adjustments easily in the few places where rules differ (as, for example, the number of times a player may bounce the ball before serving it). The greatest changes lie in the

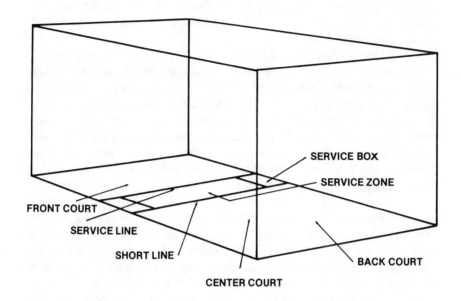

FRONT COURT

SERVICE LINE

SHORT LINE

CENTER COURT

SERVICE BOX

SERVICE ZONE

BACK COURT

Diagram of the racquetball (and handball) court.

choice of either a stringed racquet or a wooden paddle for the striking implement and the resulting problems of control. Racquetball also uses a slightly larger ball than paddleball which affects the speed and bounce. But it takes advanced and expert players to utilize these differences.

It would be foolish to say that paddleball will be supplanted by racquetball, for there is plenty of room for both games, their players and their fans. Because of the remarkable surge in popularity of racquetball, the present work focusses in this chapter on racquetball.

The Game

Racquetball is a game of constant motion, intensive concentration on movement of the ball, and dominant court position—in other words, anticipation.

In its most popular form it is played by two or four players, on an indoor rectangular four-walled court. The court is 20 feet wide, 20 feet high, and 40 feet long, with a back wall at least 12 feet high. Walls

and ceiling are often concrete but the floor must be wood. Entrance to
the court is through a door at the back, set flush with the wall. Some
courts have side entrances.

There are but four lines on the court floor, and only two of
these apply to singles play. Midway on the 40 foot length a line (the
short line) is drawn between the sidewalls, thus dividing the space into
the front and back courts. Five feet in front of this line and paralleling
it is another line (the service line). The area thus marked is the service
zone. In doubles play two more lines 18 inches from and parallel to the
side walls mark off service boxes. Two more lines are often drawn on
the side walls five feet behind the short line to show where the receiving
team must stand during the service.

A ball is played against the walls and ceiling using a small
stringed racquet. The serving side may win a point by serving an ace,
winning a rally, or profiting by the receiving side's error. The receiving
side may earn the right to serve (although with no point awarded) by
winning a rally or profiting from the serving side's error. The first side
to score 21 points wins a game. The first side to win two games wins a
match. The USRA uses an 11-point game called a "tie breaker" for the
deciding third game.

The singles and doubles games are official forms of racquetball
competition, recognized by the USRA and the NRC. All associations
divide players by age groups with separate men's and women's events.
The official rules sanction no events for mixed doubles or competition
between men and women although both forms of play are popular on
an informal basis.

An abridged form of the USRA rules is included at the end of
the chapter.

Equipment

Racquet

The rules specify that the maximum head length is 11 inches and
the width nine inches. The handle may not exceed seven inches in
length. The racquet must include a thong which is wrapped securely
around the player's wrist for safety purposes. The strings may be gut,
monofilament, nylon, or metal. The racquet itself may be made of any
material. A typical weight for a metal racquet is 9½ ounces. Four
major manufacturers of official racquets are the General Sportcraft

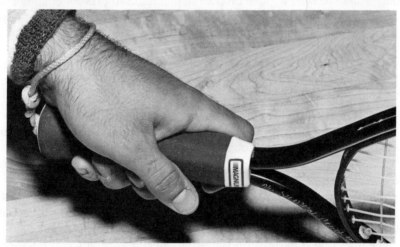

Top: The forehand grip (the traditional handshake grasp with fingers well extended along the handle). Bottom: The backhand grip has the hand more on top of the handle. The wrist band is worn by this left-hander and many others to control moisture. The thong around the wrist is required by the rules for safety.

Company, the Marcraft Recreation Corporation, the Ektelon Company, and Leach Industries.

Ball

The official ball shall be 2¼ inches in diameter, weigh approximately 1.4 ounces and bounce 67–72 inches from a 100-inch drop at a temperature of 76° F. The approved ball is the Seamco 558 manufactured by the Seamco Rubber Company.

Clothing

In tournament play the rules specify a basic uniform type that will not interfere with the player's ability to follow the flight of a small dark ball in a white room. For practice racquetball players wear a wide variety of casual sports clothing. You might see loosely fitting T-shirts made still looser by the removal of one sleeve, or a range of footwear, right down to bare feet. Since the game is extremely vigorous and is played indoors, most players elect to wear shorts, light tops, and comfortable gym shoes with good nonslip tread. Some players like to wear a glove on the racquet hand to prevent chafing and slipping. Wrist and head bands are popular for controlling sweat. Eye guards are also recommended for players.

Play of the Ball

The ball is put in play by the server who stands within the service zone, bounces the ball, and hits it to the front wall. The rebound of the ball must be strong enough to carry it behind the short line to the back court. If the ball is illegally served the server has one more chance to make it a legal serve.

The receiver has the option of striking the ball either on the fly or after the first bounce and before the ball touches the floor a second time. The receiver may return the ball directly to the front wall or angle it so that it caroms off the walls or ceiling, in any combination. The only requirement is that the ball reach the front wall at some time before it touches the floor. Then it is the server's turn to hit.

Experienced players use a variety of strokes (forehand, backhand, and overhand), at different speeds to catch their opponents off-guard and at several angles or movement patterns to drive their opponents deeper right or left. Service returns include the drive (a hard-hit response to a fast ball, intended to speed the ball past the server), the ceiling return (to hit a shot like the lob to the ceiling before rebounding to the front wall), the kill (designed to hit the ball so low on the front wall it will be difficult for the server to attack), the z-ball (a ball which rebounds from front wall to side wall to opposite side wall without touching the floor), and the around-the-wall (a ball that rebounds first from a side wall, then the front wall, then goes to the side opposite the one from which it was first struck). Offensive shots are the kill (four varieties to end play of the ball by making it die on the floor), the drop (to create a very weak rebound), and various passes to place the ball too far beyond the opponent. Defensive shots are the ceiling ball (which should have spin), the lob (a high ball hit softly and firmly), and the z- and around-the-wall balls. *Inside Racquetball* by Chuck Leve (Henry Regnery Co., Chicago, 1973) gives excellent descriptions of these plays that are valuable to students of the game. Most of these shots may be attempted by the beginner in the course of the first or second lesson.

Players who come to racquetball after developing skills in other racquet sports (such as squash or racquets) are able to take over the game at the start and achieve instant success at a gratifying level. Experience in tennis and badminton also gives a good background for early success in racquetball. The similarities in racquet, grip, stance, balance, eye-hand-racquet-ball coordination, court moves and game strategy quickly make the new player feel at home. Progress is greatly enhanced by this confidence.

Fundamentals

Forehand

The racquet is held in the traditional handshake grip used in most racquet sports, with the lower edge of the racquet pointing to the floor and face of the racquet perpendicular. The hand is well spread along the grip, the forefinger curled in an extended position which gives more control. Of course the shortened striking implement necessitates having the end of the grip much closer to the palm of the hand than in other sports.

In the ideal forehand stroke the right-handed player addresses the ball with the upper left side of the body turned toward the target, weight well back on the right foot, knees bent, both feet on the floor, right arm well back and wrist cocked. The stroke is executed with a full arm sweep; the right shoulder drops, the wrist cock lessens, the weight shifts from the right foot to left foot as the arm travels and the follow-through completes the movement. At the moment of impact the ball is met squarely just about opposite the left toe. Arm and wrist are fully extended and the power generated by the weight shift and arm sweep is at its fullest. (The mirror image of these techniques describes the left-handed player's approach to each stroke.)

Most important to successful performance is the player's intense concentration on the ball, complete to the moment of impact.

Backhand

Most players prefer to shift the grip slightly, turning the racquet face approximately two inches in a clockwise direction so that the top edge of the racquet is positioned toward the target. As the ball approaches, the right side is now toward it, the arm with the wrist cocked is back across the body, and the weight is on the left foot.

In executing the stroke, the player makes the weight transfer by stepping toward the ball with the right foot. On impact the ball is met farther toward the target than in the forehand stroke and the follow-through is high.

Overhand

Most players use the forehand grip for this stroke. Generally the stroke resembles the performance given with a flyswatter when trying to reach a bothersome insect flying just above the head. The body is squared to the target rather than sideways, and the stroke has wrist action to force the ball toward the intended target. It is the most difficult stroke to control but can be used effectively in making kill shots.

Courtesies

Court etiquette is important even in so robust and casual a game as racquetball and in spite of the fact that many forms of gamesmanship are not disallowed. Guidelines to courtesy are based on safety and are well enforced by the rules section which deals with hindering an opponent from making a play. Forbidden conduct includes wild swinging, intentional denying of an opponent's chance to see or return a ball, and deliberate shoving or pushing. An avoidable hinder gives your opponent a point or the serve. There is a replay if the hinder is unavoidable or if you have checked your swing (which might have hit an opponent) and have called a "safety hinder."

Opposite: The forehand sequence (here by a lefthander).

Rules

The following rules of racquetball are highly abridged and informally worded. Current official rules sanctioned by the USRA are easily available on request from racquetball sports centers, sporting goods stores, and manufacturers of racquetball equipment.

The serve

The server is decided by mutual agreement or by toss. The server may serve from any place in the serving zone. The ball is bounced and struck so that the first rebound is from the front wall. A legal serve requires that the ball, should it land, be behind the short line. In doubles, the server's partner must be in one of the service boxes at the side. The server has two chances to make a legal serve. If both serves are fault the other side now takes over the serve. In doubles the server's partner takes over except at the start of each game, when the first team to serve has only one turn.

There are many kinds of defective serves that are disallowed in order to keep the game fair for both sides. It does not take much playing experience to understand the unacceptability of: ball hitting partner (in doubles play), unintentional screening of a view of the ball by the serving side, server leaving service zone too early, ball not reaching the short line on the first rebounded bounce, ball rebounding from a side wall before the front wall, ball hitting the ceiling immediately after rebounding from the front wall, ball rebounding from front wall immediately to back wall.

Return of service

The receiver must stand at least five feet back of the short line and stay there until the ball passes this line. On a legal return the ball must be struck either on the fly or after the first bounce. It may be returned directly to the front wall, or may touch any of the other walls and ceiling on its way. It may not touch the floor before it reaches the front wall. Failure to return a serve or to win an ensuing rally after a good return results in a point for the server.

The server continues to serve until some playing error against the serving side results in the end of play. At this time the serve goes to

Opposite: The backhand sequence.

In a forehand drive the player moves quickly to address the ball, racquet well back, and side of body to the target for full power on the hit.

the opposing side (except in doubles where two servers first have their turns) and no point is awarded. The game ends when one side has 21 points.

Other rules are concerned with special conditions unique to racquetball. For example, because of the safety rule requiring a wrist thong, players are not allowed to switch the racquet from one hand to the other; however, two-handed strokes are legal. "Hinders" are clearly defined, as has been mentioned. Provision is made for emergency in the case of a damp ball or an injury. Rules for time-out and delaying the game are included. Official rules guides also include a section discussing tournaments, with provisions for draws, scheduling, rankings, and general management.

Professional Racquetball

The opportunities for earning a living as a racquetball player are generally limited to prize money from professional tournaments and to promotional activities peripheral to actual play. Like squash racquets, the game itself cannot be viewed in a gymnasium or stadium because of the four-walled enclosure required by the sport. Only a few people can observe live-action play from the small gallery above the end wall of the court. Even the addition of glass viewpoints along the sides of the court do not open the game to a live audience.

The requirements of court construction must give primary consideration to the rebound of the ball and to providing a background against which the players can see the ball. Technologically it is possible to build courts of glass. Southfield, in Detroit, has two courts in which three walls are glass. About 600 spectators can be seated there, but a ticket sale of 600 cannot provide a base for prize money needed in professional tournaments. As the popularity of the game grows, promoters of professional racquetball are looking to television for the spectators and to private industry for funding. Television is reaching an ever-enlarging audience of players and fans while companies specializing in sports equipment are financing professional tours.

At present the top twenty professional players have comfortable incomes from prize money, endorsements, exhibition games, instructional clinics, and other promotional work. But for most racquetball enthusiasts, racquetball remains a participant sport for the amateur.

Organizations

The National Handball Association (NHA)
  4101 Dempster St
  Skokie IL 60076

The National Paddleball Association (NPA)
  Sports Building, University of Michigan
  Ann Arbor MI 48104

The National Racquetball Club
  4101 Dempster St
  Skokie IL 60076

The United States Racquetball Association (USRA)
  4101 Dempster St
  Skokie IL 60076
  (Publishes *National Racquetball*)

Chapter 8

Badminton

History

Badminton presents the interested student of racquet sports with a plethora of information but only as far back as 1873. "The game played at Badminton," as it first came to be called, must have been something of a social coup when the Duke of Beaufort presented it to his guests at his home in Badminton, Gloucestershire, England. One source of information states that the game evolved from the ancient children's game of battledore-and-shuttlecock, implying an English or European background for the game. Another states that badminton itself was played in India previous to the Duke of Beaufort's successful party, so it could have been brought to England by army officers previously stationed in India. At any rate, the Duke's guests (How many of them were there? Who were they?) apparently were so beguiled by the new activity that they spread the game and the name, badminton, throughout the fashionable set of army officers and ranking public servants of the British Empire, including India. Or so it would seem. Laws of the game were first drawn up in Poona, India, that same year. Even now, one will read occasionally that badminton came from a game called "poona," and possibly it was first found by British soldiering in that city. But in trying to trace earlier origins, even to find a clear description of "battledore-and-shuttlecock," the researcher embarks on a worldwide Odyssey filled with conjecture and unanswered questions.

The venerable *Encyclopaedia Britannica*, for example, identifies the game with Greek drawings (which depict people at play using

122

The modern racquet is extremely light in weight (about five ounces) and very whippy, as befits the most vigorous of the racquet sports.

racquets and shuttlecocks), then states that it was popular in the Far East and has known centuries of play by children in Europe. The encyclopaedia then goes no further in describing the game other than to conclude that badminton was a further development of battledore-

and-shuttlecock, thus closing the questing circle, so to speak. Only by digging into more specific studies on the anthropology of play can one discover that "the game played at Badminton" is just another example of the universality of sport forms, like all the other racquet sports described in this book. Overwhelming evidence of racquets being used to strike shuttles is found throughout the whole world.

For instance, the Indians in the northwestern portion of North America used small wooden racquets to keep a shuttlecock in the air. A circle game, it was played by a large group according to a special formula describing the progression of turns and seemed to be used as some form of ritual. Evidence of this game goes back to pre-Columbian times. Racquets have also been found on the San Pedro River in the Southwest corner of New Mexico, dating from A.D. 900. In South America, in northern Peru, a ceremonial badminton-like ritual was discovered by Dr. Gerdt Kutcher of Berlin. Reported in Copenhagen in 1956, at the 32nd Congress of the National Congress of Americanists, Dr. Kutcher's paper on "The Ceremonial Badminton in the Ancient Culture of Mochica" caused a considerable stir among the students of ceremonial play patterns. (Why is it that certain play forms seem to repeat themselves, even though no communications among widely separated civilizations could reasonably have been expected to exist?)

Finally, in the Orient (China, Japan, and East Asia), more badminton-like games appear. First described by Steward Colin in 1895 as "Games of Korea with notes on the Corresponding Games of China and Japan" (republished under the title "Games of the Orient," Charles E. Tuttle, Rutland, Vt., 1958), these games have been traced back to the 5th century B.C. and persist in some form today. How and when they reached India can best be explained through the ageless trade routes which lay between India and the Orient. The peoples of these lands borrowed back and forth in culture as well as in trade. A citizen of one or another civilization must have been the first to stuff feathers into a lump of clay, or a large seed pod, or a piece of wood and swat it up into the air.

Turn-of-the-century kits for playing at battledore-and-shuttlecock included feathered shuttles that were considerably larger and heavier than their modern counterparts. The racquets, or bats, were short-handled, the striking surfaces made of parchment stretched over a narrow hoop, leaving a hollow space between. No net was used in the game.

Even though it is known that this sort of play seems to exist throughout the world, the addition of a recognizable net may be another matter. Perhaps that is what the Duke of Beaufort added when he "introduced" the game of badminton. Perhaps someone in India had borrowed a net from the tennis of the day. At any rate, as previously stated, Poona, India, was the place where modern "laws of badminton" were first promulgated. Back in England again, 20 years later, in 1892, at Southsea, Hampshire, the playing court was finally standardized, a uniform set of laws adopted, and a Badminton Association formed. In 1899, the Association was ready to present its first All-England Championship: the world tournament for its day.

By World War I, the game had become a favorite throughout Great Britain. Other nations also found badminton to their liking. Badminton was played in the United States during the 1890s and reached its first peak of popularity in 1929.

Even though there were enthusiastic players in the New World, not until 1936 was the American Badminton Association formed. This organization changed its name to the United States Badminton Association in 1982.

Now, in the United States, the strongest support for the sport is still on the Pacific coast. It has always been a so-called minor sport in the United States, but it continues to grow, even flourishing to the point of producing players of international calibre, including at least one world champion.

The Game

Badminton has been accurately described as a game of perpetual motion, unmatched for speed, dexterity, endurance, and action. This is the game as played by advanced and expert players, particularly those interested in competition. There is another form of play enjoyed by thousands who confine their efforts to moves which resemble a formalized game of pattycake — games which probably depict the ancient ritualistic forms of badminton with some degree of accuracy. Nevertheless, badminton, as played in competition, is by far the most vigorous of the racquet sports.

The game is played by two players (singles), or four players (doubles), who volley a small feathered cork ball (shuttlecock), back and forth across a net, using long, lightweight, stringed racquets. The net is high, measuring 5 feet 1 inch at the posts, and an even five feet at the center. The court dimensions are 44 by 17 feet for singles play. Doubles adds a 1½ foot alley on each side, increasing the width to 20 feet. Lines for service areas are the only other markings on the court.

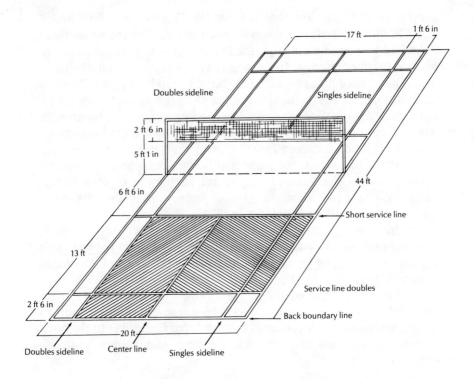

Diagram of badminton court.

Badminton may be enjoyed either outdoors or indoors, but only the indoor form of the game offers real competition. The shuttlecock is so light and so responsive that even the slightest air currents disturb its flight, thus outdoor play can never hope to equal the excitement of the indoor game. Unfortunately, far too many indoor facilities are hampered by low ceilings, but the enthusiastic player makes the best of it in trying to learn the game. Thousands of older gyms and game rooms have ceilings far below the standard clearances specified in the rules: 26 feet for international play, and 30 feet for many national organizations.

Badminton differs most specifically from its companion racquet sports in that the cork "ball" used in the game carries a formal arrangement of feathers so that all returns are volleys. There are no shots taken after a bounce. Furthermore, spin cannot be imparted to this feathered missile (sometimes called "shuttle" or "bird"). The feathers impart peculiar characteristics to the trajectory of the bird as compared with those of the spherical balls used in other sports. In general, the shuttlecock flies to the point where most forward momentum is lost, then plummets toward the court. (Exceptions are found in smash and kill shots which purposely are directed to the floor.) The timing in the game allows no rest periods such as those where a ball may be taking a relatively slow or easy bounce.

Even in the quick, flurried exchanges between advanced players, the shuttle may cross the net a dozen or more times before the point is decided, when opponents are evenly matched. The shots are mixed in order to draw the opponent out of position, to set up a winning play. Forehand and backhand stroking is used to produce drives, clears (equivalent to lobs), drop shots, and smashes.

Badminton appears to be equally popular when played as singles or doubles. Men's and women's singles and doubles and also mixed doubles comprise the competition, both nationally and internationally. It is another game in which the newcomer can find instant success and fun in patting the shuttle back and forth to an opponent. Hard work and practice make the next move to the real game.

Equipment

The racquet

Badminton racquets have no restrictions laid upon them by the rules, but they have evolved into extremely lightweight, whippy forms, almost standardized. Once made entirely of wood, they now are usually all metal or a combination of wood and metal. A typical racquet is 26 inches long with a nearly round head measuring 8¼ inches wide. Weights vary from 3¼ to 5¼ ounces.

Racquets are manufactured by several of the long established sporting goods companies. At present ranked players appear to be favoring the Yonex and Kawasaki (Japanese), the Carlton (English), and the Dunlop and Fort.

The shuttlecock

The official shuttlecock is made of cork, 1 to 1⅛ inches in diameter, covered with kid leather. The striking surface is hemispherical; the opposite end is flattened. From this flat base protrude 16 goose feathers, 2½ to 2¾ inches long, which flare to a 2½

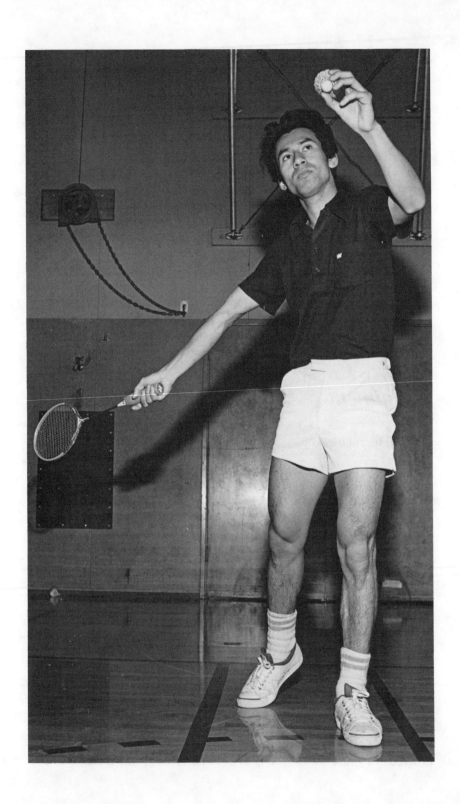

Opposite and above: The standard serve sequence, showing one method for holding the shuttle, followed by the stroke as the shuttle is dropped.

inch diameter at the end. They are arranged in a symmetrical overlapping pattern and are tied into place with string near the base. Shuttles are also made of nylon. Some are purposely heavier in weight for outdoor use. The indoor birds weigh 73 to 85 grains.

Popular brands which are also used in official tournament play are the Victor, H-L, RSL, and General Sportcraft. Shuttles are made in various grades, such as premium and champion. Some firms also manufacture nylon birds, which last longer than the feathered ones, and are favored by schools on the basis of economics. Shuttles are not very costly, to be sure, but a hard-played contest can go through several in a match.

Clothing

Tradition has long decreed that badminton matches should be played in white clothing, although players practice in a variety of athletic garb. Television coverage prefers colors on the players, although the All-England Tournament still specifies white. The United States national tournaments allow color, as do other international matches. Standard tennis wear is the preferred choice of most players. Shoes are tennis shoes of the player's choice.

Play of the Shuttlecock

The shuttle is put in play by the server who must stand with both feet contacting the floor within the service court during delivery. The shuttle is dropped, then hit across the net to the receiver who waits within the boundaries of the service court diagonally opposite the server. The shuttle is then volleyed back and forth across the net until some error or unreturnable shot ends the play. Only the server may score points; the receiver earns the right to serve should the rally end in the receiver's favor. Game score is 11 for women's singles events, and 15 for all other events. In certain handicap matches, the score may be 21 points. Matches are the best two out of three games.

The serve is basic to good performance in badminton. Because only the server (or "hand-in"), may score points, the shuttle must be put in play so that the receiver (or "hand-out"), does not have too great an advantage in making a return. The shuttle is, therefore, delivered either very high and deep (the long serve), thus forcing the opponent back; or extremely close to the net and shallow (the short serve), thereby drawing the opponent forward. Because of differing

The "ready" position from which a player awaits the serve.

This preparation could result in either a smash or a drop shot. Note how the elbow leads and the wrist cocks, essentials for good play.

service areas in the doubles and singles games, the long serve is most often used in singles and the short serves are used most often in doubles. (The doubles service court is 2½ feet shorter and 1½ feet wider than the singles service court.)

Two more basic strokes are the drive and the clear. In the former, the shuttle is struck with great force, at about head or full racquet extension level, the idea being to angle the shot to pull an opponent out of position. The latter shot is a defensive shot, acting as a lob does in the other racquet games. The clear is directed extremely high and deep, being aimed so that it would land within the last six to 12 inches of the court should it fall. It is designed to break up an offense by forcing the opponent to retreat far back.

The smash, or kill, is (as the name suggests) one that effectively puts away the point. The shuttle is angled sharply to the floor. The drop shot is also a winner. In this stroke, the shuttle is met with a damped impact so that it barely floats across the net.

Advanced badminton players use an astonishing mix of these different strokes in their matches. Doubles play sees even more variety, for here the court is covered by two players on a side. The swift changes of pace, the shifting of partners from side-by-side to up-and-back to diagonal positions present a bewildering show of teamwork to the observer. But to the seasoned badminton player, the game is like a ballet in presto time: a game for the superbly conditioned athlete.

Of all the racquet games, perhaps badminton carries the most misconceptions regarding the influence of its techniques on those of other games. There is a persistent belief that the basic wristiness of all badminton strokes will harm a player's performance in other games, particularly tennis. However it does not require a great deal of insight to understand that the differences in racquet weights, timing, and performance of ball versus shuttlecock are so great that scant deleterious carry-over can occur. It takes but a few minutes of warmup time for players experienced in badminton and any of the other racquet sports to resume the moves characteristic of the game at hand. Indeed, the common denominator of all racquet sports—eye-hand coordination, endurance, and game strategy based on placement of angled shots—have far more positive than negative carry-over value. Only in the most advanced levels of competition, wherein a player specializes in one sport and aspires to reach the top of the competitive world, might a legitimate claim be made against playing more than one racquet sport. All else is mind-set.

Fundamentals

Forehand and backhand grip

The racquet is held in a modified handshake grip, with the edge

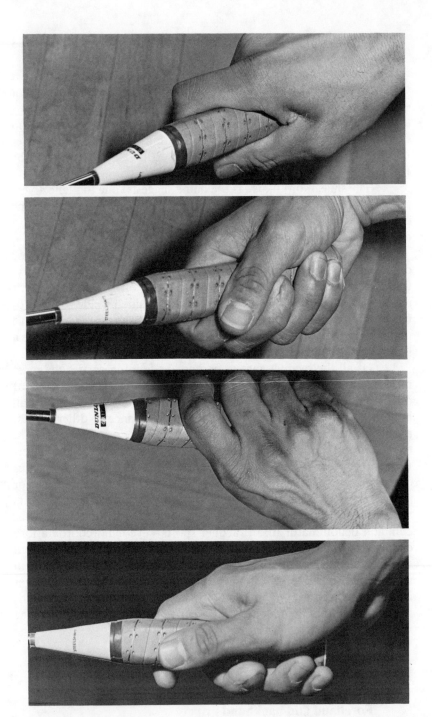

Top: Forehand grip viewed from side and top. Bottom: Backhand grip, from side and top.

of the stringed face toward the floor. The fingers of the hand are in a fist-like alignment, rather than spread along the grip. The butt of the handle presses slightly into the heel of the hand — in other words, the grip may be said to be quite the opposite of a choked grip (although children sometimes choke up a bit until they develop enough strength). This allows for maximum whip in the wristiness of badminton strokes.

In the backhand, the racquet is rotated an inch or two clockwise, thus placing the hand more on top. Most players brace the thumb up along the back of the handle for the backhand.

Because of the lightness of the racquet, no assistance from the free hand is necessary to flip the racquet about from one grip to another. Only a little practice is needed in releasing and moving the racquet position with a slight tossing motion before the whole operation becomes almost instinctively automatic.

The serve

In the long serve, the right-handed player stands in a stride position, left foot forward, weight on the left foot. The shuttle is held at the throat or by the feathers directly in front of the server, cork facing downward. The racquet may be held up or back of the player, in a neutral position. The serving move begins with the right arm travelling rearward, bringing the racquet head back in a sharp wrist cock. Weight remains stable, or transfers slightly to the rear foot. On delivery the racquet hand is brought forward as the shuttle is dropped, the heel of the racquet handle leading. The head is brought forward with a sharp whipping action to meet the bird. Impact is well in front of the player, the arc travelling in an upward direction. Follow-through is high, extended toward the target or around the body. Although this description concentrates on arm movement, there is powerful body action brought into play by twisting of hips and torso. The rules of badminton do not allow the server to lift the feet to step into a serve, therefore weight transfer must occur through this intense twisting motion.

The player may stand anywhere within the service court, but the best position is close to the center line and about a racquet's length back from the short service line.

For the short serve, the stance and action imitate that of the long serve. The difference comes at the moment just before impact when the player damps the speed of racquet head and gently impels the bird over the net. There is no body behind the stroke. The follow-through of the racquet head is low, pointing toward the target. To be

effective, the short serve must clear the net no higher than a few inches. Anything more than nine or ten inches results in a floating shot that sets up a smash return from the receiver.

There is another short serve, a fairly recent innovation, which is used in doubles by many advanced players. In this serve, the receiver fully expects a short serve. The server stands close to the short service line, feet apart, body facing the net. The racquet is held in front of the body in a backhand grip, with the hand at shoulder level and the racquet head pointing directly downward to the floor. The free hand holds the shuttle at arm's length in front of the body, in the direction of the target. Some players tense their leg muscles and rise upward on their toes as they prepare for the stroke, thus enabling themselves to spring directly into action on the return.

The shuttle is dropped and the stroke is executed by a quick forward move of the racquet head, emanating from a wrist movement. Because the racquet face travels only about 12 inches before reaching the bird, as opposed to the full swing described in the other short serve, this serve is an extremely deceptive stroke.

Both of these short serves are chiefly used in doubles play.

Clears

The underhand clear stroke is executed much like the long serve but without the restriction on footwork. The player steps into the stroke with full power. In the overhand clear, the shuttle is met with the racquet face slightly angled toward the ceiling, so as to direct the bird high and far back. Clears are usually taken on the forehand, the stronger side, although accomplished players can also execute the backhand clear.

Drives

In both the forehand and the backhand drive, the shuttle is met at shoulder level or a bit above. The heel of the hand leads the stroke. The racquet head is whipped around to meet the bird with full power. In the "round-the-head" drive, a spectacular stroke, the racquet meets the shuttle on the backhand side of the player but with the forehand side of the racquet. This stroke is used when a high drive is needed and when it could be taken by a normal backhand swing. The racquet is

Opposite, left and right: The short serve, sideview. Note the restricted racquet movement and how the shuttlecock barely clears the net.

Opposite and above: In the "round-the-head" drive, the whip-like motion of the racquet imparts tremendous speed to the shuttle.

brought up to shoulder level as though for a forehand, then flung around the head to meet the shuttle. It is a far less difficult stroke to master than it looks, and is usually more effective than a backhand.

Smash or kill

This stroke is used when the opponent sets up a high, lazy floater in the middle of the court, usually as a result of successful maneuvering from the other side. The shuttle is met high and in front of the player, at full arm extension. The racquet face angles toward the floor. The bird should barely clear the net and travel at such an angle that it strikes the floor before it can be returned. The wrist leads throughout the windup to the smash. Execution is, once more, with great wrist power.

The drop shot

The drop is the great deceiver in badminton, requiring cleverness in acting for perfect execution. The moves preceding the drop shot mimic those used before the kill, and are intended to alert the opponent to a hard-hit return. At the last moment, the movement of the racquet is slowed, the impact of string on shuttle damped, and the bird barely floats across the net. Should the opponent successfully pick up a drop shot, a smash is often set up for the next response.

Footwork

There are, of course, basic footwork patterns in badminton—left side to net for forehand, right side for backhand—but the speed of the game often finds the player scrambling with no formal attention paid to the set of feet. In general, the sliding steps of the so-called "basketball shuffle" are fundamental to good play: steps which avoid crossing the feet in a gravevine pattern. Also a good long-reaching lunge step with quick return to the center court position is likely to be more effective than short, running steps. Even so, in advanced play, a great deal of scampering appears to take place on the court.

Opposite: The player lunges to retrieve a drop shot.

Courtesies

High standards of courteous behavior are the custom on the badminton court. There is very little observable gamesmanship. Bad temper and ill nature, from player or gallery, are not considered to be good form or in keeping with the spirit of the game.

Rules

Court dimensions differ slightly in singles and doubles play. (See diagram.) The most important difference is in the matter of the doubles service courts. The serve may use the extension granted by the alleys, but a doubles long serve line cuts off 2½ feet from the rear of the court. The beginner in badminton is reminded that after delivery of the serve, the entire court service is in-bounds.

The serve must be delivered so that at the moment of impact, the head of the racquet is discernibly below the wrist and the shuttle is below the waist.

In scoring, the women's singles games go to 11 points. At a score of nine-all, the game may be "set" for three points. This is the option of the person not serving when the tie occurs. A similar option occurs at 10-all, when the game may be set for two points. Women's doubles and men's events go to 15 points. The score may be set at 13-all for five points, at 14-all for three points.

Special rules exist for doubles play involving court position in serving and receiving. Each member of a doubles team serves (has the "hand") until that team (the "in" team) loses a rally. In other words, there are two "hands" in every "inning." However, because only the serving side may score points, it is considered too great an advantage to give two hands to the first inning. Therefore, this inning has only one hand. Service should be decided by toss of a coin, although often this toss is accomplished by the spin of a racquet.

Rules also define faulty serves, errors in play, and "lets" for replays. In general, the "Laws of Badminton" are simple to understand and easy to interpret.

Professional Badminton

Badminton competition seems to be growing both in quality and quantity. In America, college scholarships are now available for talented players. Coaches and physical educators can supplement their incomes if they can teach badminton. Manufacturers of equipment are generous in supplying racquets, birds, and clothing to top players. But, as yet, there is no real way to make a living in badminton as a playing professional.

Of course, there are dreams of the sport's opening up to the public, particularly through television coverage. But there are difficult problems met in covering the game through TV. These are related to the curious foreshortening of the court brought about by the television lens, and the difficulty of getting camera angles to pick up the play. Although one sees occasional television specials featuring high level play, the fact is that badminton is a lot more exciting to play than to watch.

Organizations

United States Badminton Association
  POB 237
  Swartz Creek MI 48473
  Cletus Eli, executive secretary

Chapter 9
Handball

History

The game of handball as played today came to the United States from Ireland with the wave of immigrants in the early 19th century. The early name of the sport in Ireland and England was "fives," thought to relate to the five fingers on the hand, even though this game used both hands and both feet (that's 20 digits in all). Records clearly trace handball back for ten centuries, but at this point the scholarship breaks down and the easy but inaccurate assumptions begin.

It is interesting to note that even with a game as uncomplicated as handball there are differing opinions as to its origin and its influence on similar games. Perhaps the very simplicity of the game has tempted people to take for granted its position in the anthropology of play. The student's ordinary sources of information often contain statements which will not bear close scrutiny.

For example, the *Encyclopedia of Sports* (compiled by the late Frank G. Menke, revised for its fifth edition by Suzanne Treat, and published by A.S. Barnes) states, "the Irish *originated* the game [of handball] in the 10th century, and this game undoubtedly was the parent of tennis" (page 537). In regard to the second part of this claim, it would be more accurate to think of handball and tennis as cousins on the family tree of sport, not as siblings and certainly not as parent and offspring. As for the first part of the statement, it is hard to credit a specific origin to the Irish in the years 900 in view of the pictures, references and archeological traces of ball games played by hand in Greek, Egyptian and Roman civilizations.

144

According to the *Encyclopaedia Britannica* (15th edition, 1979) "one of the oldest games played with a ball, handball, has been traced back to the *thermae* or baths of Rome." Subsequent prowling through the volumes of the encyclopedia bring forth no description of these *thermae* and no other mention of ancient handball. However, the article continues by calling handball "the forerunner of modern jai alai," a statement immediately open to question since jai alai uses an implement for propelling a ball. (A more logical assumption is that the game descends from tennis, racquets, and *la soule*. See Chapter 1.)

In the presence of all these conjectures it is refreshing to return to the rather well kept records of the sport of handball in modern times. Fives has been mentioned as its antecedent. The game is still played today in England in three versions, two of which even have league play between schools and formal associations for governance.

Eton fives is played nowadays in British public schools. This form of the game of handball is believed to have originated in the casual play of children hitting a ball against any convenient wall. Eton fives is quite a complicated game. It is played in a court that is a copy of the Eton College Chapel playing area. This area includes a step, angled ledges, a small butress, a cavity called the "Dead Man's Hole" and is enclosed on three sides. Only the doubles game is played, two players to a side. Game score is 12. The serving side wins points; the receiving side wins the right to serve after winning two rallies in a row—a feature unique to this game. Hand or wrist hits are legal. Gloves are worn. It is a bewildering game to watch. The league competition is under the Eton Fives Association.

The second fives game currently played is called Rugby fives. It too is played in the British public schools. Unlike the Eton court, the Rugby court has plain walls, and the front wall includes a two and a half foot modified tell-tale. The ball may be hit with hand or forearm. Under the control of the Rugby Fives Association, this version of the game is by far the most popular.

The third game is called Winchester fives. It is similar to Rugby fives but the left side wall is placed at an angle thus making the back part of the court narrower than the front and causing some interesting rebounds. No institutional association is connected with this version of the game, but it is said that Winchester fives players adapt quite easily to the Rugby form of the game.

Even though these versions of the game of fives still are played, handball itself in the four-wall version is the popular game of today. In Ireland, more than 100 years ago, one Mehan Baggs gave the game a great push forward when he learned how to control the ball by putting spin on it. Another famous player was John Cavanagh of St. Giles who played in the late 18th and early 19th centuries. But the greatest impetus to the game in the United States was given by Phil Casey who came to this country in 1882.

Settling in Brooklyn, Casey was appalled to discover that a sort of one-wall handball game was played against any walls that were convenient, but that no real handball courts were in existence. So in 1886 he built one of his own. It was a huge court by today's standards, measuring 65 by 35 feet with a front wall 30 feet high. But the game in those days was different too, since it permitted kicking the ball as well as striking it with the hands. Casey was an avid sportsman. He defeated Bernard McQuade, another migrant from Ireland, in 1887 or 1888, calling this game the championship of America. Next he challenged John Lawlor, Ireland's undisputed leading player, to a world championship. The winner would have to take 11 games, the first 10 to be played in Ireland. Casey travelled to Ireland where he lost six of the 10, but when Lawlor came to America Casey won the next seven straight and four more for good measure. Phil Casey retired in 1900, still champion.

Soon after, interest in the game declined. It was kept alive by the Amateur Athletic Union and gradually came back, chiefly because of interest in the one-wall game. Playgrounds and swimming areas put in outdoor backboards. Some even had folding sides which could convert the court into a kind of three-walled court. The armed forces used handball as part of its fitness training. And as the one-wall game grew in popularity so did the four-wall game.

In 1919 the first National Senior AAU four-wall championship was held in Los Angeles. In 1924 a one-wall championship was held in New York. In 1951 the United States Handball Association was formed, at last bringing together the different groups which had kept the sport going. These were the Amateur Athletic Union (1919), the Young Men's Christian Association (1925) and the National Jewish Welfare Board. In 1959 these four groups met to standardize the rules. The game is still seeking national recognition through the USHA.

Modern rules are almost the same as the rules were in the 1880's, but, of course, no foot shots are allowed. The ball has developed from the extremely hard ball used years ago in Ireland, through a hollow ball (a tennis ball with the cover removed), to a lively hollow black ball of the 1930's, the forerunner of the ball used today.

Nowadays there are millions of handball players. The most popular version of the sport is played indoors, the four-walled game, although in reality it is *five* walls for the ceiling is in bounds too. The

Handball is a game of ambidexterity and eyes on the ball.

modern handball court is identical to that used for racquetball, and
the facilities are used by players of both sports, a great boon to both
games. Handball players generally find no difficulty in quickly
mastering the game of racquetball; however, the reverse is not usually
the case.

The Game

Stamina and endurance are probably the two most important
basics of the game of handball, for it has the reputation of being one
of the most vigorous of sports, physically demanding and totally
exhausting. The casual spectator might well doubt the truth of this
statement. There is not much noise on a handball court. When the
hand meets the ball, even for the hardest hit, the sound is just a little
pat. The ball seems to travel almost in slow motion. Most rebounds
look large and long. The players seem to have all kinds of time to get
into position to make their plays. They move, for the most part, skill-
fully, in a kind of ballet, striking the ball with either hand and with
consummate grace.

But after a while, not more than five minutes, it becomes ap-
parent to the spectator that the players must be working awfully hard.
Their faces gleam with perspiration. The terry cloth sweat bands,
which protect their eyes from the sheets of moisture running down
their faces, are soaked and must be changed. The backs of their shirts
are dark with moisture. Droplets appear on the floor. And the ball
must be repeatedly dried off, for it has picked up a lot of the sweat
which now drenches the contestants.

It is not surprising that the uninitiated spectator wonders where
all this effort is coming from. A few lessons in the sport are all that are
needed to take away this sense of wonder. Handball is a game of
downright hard work.

Modern four-wall handball is most often played indoors in an
enclosure measuring 20 by 40 feet. The front wall and ceiling are also
20 feet high; the back wall must be at least 12 feet high. Floors are
usually of wood, but walls are white painted concrete. Lines on the
floor mark the service zone and a restraining area for the receiver. The
court is identical to the racquetball court. (See illustration on page
111.)

In the game itself a small rubber ball is struck with the hand or
fist against a wall, the idea being to make the ball rebound in such a
way that the opposition cannot return it.

Equipment for handball is minimal: gloves and a ball (the one on the right). The ball on the left is larger and is for racquetball.

Symmetry is the rule in this game, far more so than in any of the other games described in this book, for the player must develop ambidexterity in the play of the ball. There is no backhand in handball.

Both singles (one against one) and doubles (two against two) games are played and a cut-throat game for three players also exists. Singles is the most popular game.

Equipment

Handball requires very little equipment. The hands of the player are the racquets of the sport. However, gloves are required by rule.

One of the main purposes of gloves is to keep sweat off the ball. Another is, of course, to protect the player's hands. Beginners usually wear thick leather gloves, padded at the palms, but more advanced players prefer soft, lighter leather gloves, feeling that they can better control the ball. Some players tape the palms of their hands before putting on the gloves. Others may wear light cotton gloves under the leather ones. Gloves must fit snugly. The wrist closure must be tight in the interests of safety.

The only other item of equipment needed is the ball.

The ball

Handballs measure about 1⅞ inches in diameter and weigh 2.3 ounces. It is interesting to compare this size and weight with that of the racquetball (see photograph) which measures 2¼ inches and weighs only 1.4 ounces. It can be seen that the modern handball, considered to be a soft ball as compared with those of the 19th century, is still a very compact ball and a hard one indeed.

It is important that the ball be kept dry during play, for a damp ball can take some very peculiar bounces. Also it is said that the ball becomes slightly livelier after it has warmed up, a degree of change that may or may not influence an advanced player's game.

The Spalding ACE handball is official for USHA tournaments.

Clothing

For competition USHA specifies shirts, shorts, sox and shoes that are clean. The colors of white, pale blue and bright yellow are allowed. However, recreational handball is played in a motley selection of clothing. Many people wear sweat suits, hoping that the added warmth will melt off a few pounds.

Shoes are, of course, of great importance. Similar to those worn in racquetball and other racquet sports, they are chosen according to the preference of the player.

Gloves are required by rule.

Safety glasses are recommended.

Play of the Ball

The ball is put in play by the server who stands anywhere in the service zone, drops the ball and hits it on the bounce. The served ball must first strike the front wall. On rebound it must hit the floor behind the shortline although it may strike a side wall on the way. A second serve is allowed if the first one is faulty.

During the serve the receiver must be five feet beyond the shortline. However the moment the server's hand meets the ball the receiver may move anywhere. This differs slightly from the racquetball rule, which

The ready position

does not allow the receiver to rush in front of the five foot marker to return a serve on the fly. There is no such prohibition in handball.

In doubles play the nonserving partner on the server's team stands in a restraining area at the side.

Serves may be delivered with either hand.

As in the other racquet sports, the ball must be returned by alternate sides or teams to the front wall before touching the floor, but it can take some detours on the way. It may be directed to a side wall, the back wall or to the ceiling or any combinations thereof, provided it does not touch the floor en route to the front wall. On rebounding from the front wall the ball may be struck on the fly (volleyed) or after one bounce.

Only the serving side may score points. Game score is 21 points.

Fundamentals

Handball is a game of all forehand strokes. Most players come to the sport clearly aware of their sidedness or handedness in executing the strokes. The nondominant side, referred to as the "off" side by handball players, is very difficult to develop for most beginners. However one of the basics in learning a manual skill concerns the phenomenon of transference. If a player faithfully practices and learns a skill on the nondominant side there is an almost magical transference of improvement to the natural or dominant side. (Good ambidextrous shooters in basketball and successful switch hitters in baseball regularly capitalize on this transference in their practicing.)

Three strokes make up the basic and classic strokes for handball.

The sidearm

Similar to a sidearm pitch in baseball, this stroke, as all the others, is executed with ample wind-up and follow-through. The player stands with toes pointed toward the side wall and eyes on the ball. Knees are bent and weight is forward. The wind-up begins as the ball approaches. The striking arm is carried back and around the player's body. Weight shifts to the back foot and the hips turn toward the back. The player steps into the forward swing as the hand moves toward the ball, and the hips rotate forward. On contact, the elbow is slightly lower than the hand and there is a wrist snap. On follow-through the hand continues its sidearm path, roughly paralleling the floor, and points toward the target of the ball.

The overarm stroke

The player faces the side wall in the same position as for the side arm stroke. As the ball approaches, the striking arm reaches back toward the floor. At this time many players point either the hand or the elbow of the nonstriking arm at the ball (which is approaching at a height above the player's head). There is a twisting bend at the waist. Body weight is back. The player steps into the swing as the striking hand is brought up and forward. Body weight now moves forward also. On contact there is a snap of the wrist and the follow-through is toward one of the walls. The overarm resembles the smash or kill performed in other racquet sports.

Opposite: The sidearm stroke sequence.

The underarm stroke

This stroke may be compared to the legal softball pitch, being executed in much the same way. The player stands facing the side wall, knees bent, weight forward as the ball approaches. On the back swing the hand is brought far back, higher than the head, as the body turns and the weight shifts backward. The player steps into the swing as the hand comes forward, travelling in a low to high arc. Contact with the ball is made close to the floor. Follow-through is high.

In all of these strokes the ball is best met at a point opposite the player's midline.

The serve

This stroke is usually a sidearm stroke or may have a bit of underarm in it. There are several different kinds of serves used by a skillful player.

The power serve is a low, hard drive and may be served from any spot in the service zone.

The alley serve is directed so as to hug one or another side wall, almost paralleling it as it rebounds. The server stands near one or another wall to deliver this serve.

Angle serves are hit in such a way that the ball rebounds from front to side wall before touching the floor.

The Z serve hits front, side, floor, then opposite side.

A lob serve touches high on the front wall and lands far back. There are several variations of the lob serve, and each requires real touch.

The overhead serve requires that the ball be dropped from head height so that the serve can be overhead.

Special skills

Players beyond the beginner stage soon learn that the center court area is like home base. They try to take possession of this territory, returning to it after each shot when possible. Successful control of this area usually means control of the game.

Advanced players put spin on the ball. In handball talk this is known as hopping the ball. A natural hop has under or back spin. The reverse hop has over or top spin. Combining hop with serves can produce some startling effects.

Opposite: The overarm stroke sequence.

Courtesies

There is a great deal of camaraderie among handball players. During informal play, customarily players call penalties against themselves. Although there is a 10 second rule, the courteous server makes sure the receiver is ready before putting the ball in play. The handball gallery is usually quiet and good natured. On the whole sportsmanship on the handball court is very good.

Rules

Basic handball rules are very simple. It is only when the player enters league competition that learning refinements become necessary.

The ball may be struck with either hand but not with wrist or forearm. Fist shots are also O.K.

Gloves are required.

Only the server can score. When the receiver wins a rally the serve changes sides and no point is awarded.

Every ball that legally touches the floor must be hit before touching the floor a second time.

Opposing players may not interfere with each other in trying to play the ball. Such interference is called a hinder. Play is stopped and the point replayed.

The formal rules of the game expand on the rules mentioned in this chapter. They are published by the United States Handball Association.

Professional Play

Professional handball had a beginning in the United States over the winter of 1973–1974 in a tour sponsored by the National Handball Club. Not much opportunity exists for a career in professional play. As in many other sports, the game is far more fun to play than to watch, and professional play needs an enthusiastic and paying audience.

Opposite: The underarm stroke sequence.

Handball in action — much more fun to play than to watch.

Organizations

United States Handball Association
  4101 Dempster St
  Skokie IL 60076

Chapter 10

Playground Racquet Sports

There are a number of "games of low organization," as physical educators and coaches say, played by children and adults today. Less formal than the sports discussed in the previous chapters, they serve many functions in the world of play. For one thing, they can be lead-up games for children who will eventually move into the more structured games and forms of competition. For another they provide fun and recreation and a pleasant workout for groups of mixed ages and abilities. And also some of these games serve to sharpen skills needed in other more formal sports.

These playground racquet sports are often part of school physical education programs and of recreation center activities. They are also played in vacant lots and back yards throughout the United States. One of the current developments in popularizing these games is the SportCourt®. The product of an idea by Dan Kotler, the first SportCourt was built in 1975. It measured 20 by 44 feet and was designed to handle several different games. Now thousands of these courts have been constructed throughout the United States and they are being built in other countries. The most popular size is 30 by 60 feet. (A full-sized tennis court is 60 by 120 feet; the savings in space and money is self evident.) With night lights, a basketball standard, a net that can be placed at several different heights, and an adjustable net rebounder, the SportCourt can provide facilities for 15 different sports and games at home. And not only home owners are putting in SportCourts. Athletic club facilities are also adding these courts for the recreational use of their membership.

Among the racquet games suitable to this kind of court are

159

The SportCourt® is growing in popularity for family ownership. Here the author demonstrates a Pickle-ball® serve.

Wacketball®, Pickle-ball®, badminton, paddle tennis, one-wall handball, and modified racquetball.

The first game, Wacketball, was patented by Kotler in the hope that it would find a following among SportCourt owners. It is a tennislike game, using shortened tennis racquets and a foam ball. Tennis rules are official for the game. However, most sporting goods stores do not carry Wacketball equipment; one must buy from the SportCourt outlet.

Pickle-ball® is another game well suited to the SportCourt, but equipment for this game is also difficult to find. A canvass of the Bay Area of San Francisco by telephone and visitation found but one outlet for pickle-ball, the SportCourt distributor in Marin County. Most sporting goods stores and toy shops had never heard of the game. One large equipment store which supplies many local school systems with athletic equipment had wooden racquets such as those used for platform tennis and paddle tennis, but none of the lightweight kind for paddle ball and pickle-ball. Information in this book about the rules of the game was adapted from an article by John A. Colgate published in the *Journal of Physical Education, Recreation, and Dance* (June, 1982), the only description of the game the author has ever read, although the game has been around for a number of years.

Perhaps the supply problem is unique to the Bay Area.

The pickle-ball game is played on a regulation badminton court, measuring 20 by 44 feet, with the net hung at a three foot height. The racquet is a lightweight wooden paddle, smaller than that used in paddle tennis but much larger than a table tennis bat. A four inch Whiffleball® is used for the ball.

The ball is put in play by an underhand serve by a player who stands behind the baseline. The ball may not be bounced but is served out of hand. The serve is made diagonally cross court to the service area where it must bounce once before being played. Only one service attempt is allowed.

Game score is 11 points. Only the serving side may score.

In pickle-ball many of the elements of a tennis-like game are present, but because of the nature of the flight of the large whiffleball the game is much slower. Some sense of court positioning, strategy and basic strokes may be learned in the game. For the most part, however, pickle-ball is just an easy way to have some fun on a court.

In searching for pickle-ball and wacketball equipment the author came upon a set of implements in a toy shop for a game called Trac-ball®. The set included two plastic bats or racquets, one four inch whiffleball and basic instructions. Each bat resembles a cut down lacrosse stick, having a basket-like cage at its end which measures about 16 x 8 inches with a four inch handle. Instructions in the kit show five different strokes but give no other information about how the game should be played. Presumably Trac-ball players do their own thing. The game was developed in 1975 by Wham-O Manufacturing Company, the same company that puts out a good line of Frisbees. It is easy to visualize an informal game of Trac-ball on a SportCourt, using the net at the five foot badminton height or even the seven foot volleyball height.

A similar game to Trac-ball may be found in the game called Hi-Li Scoop®. This is another toy shop plastic special, manufactured by COSOM as one of its Safe-T-Play® products. The racquets in this game are plastic scoops which frankly imitate jai-alai bats. The ball is a four inch whiffleball. Casual rules suggest a net placed at volleyball height. No more rules are given.

The most formal racquet game to be played on a SportCourt may well be paddle tennis even though the regulation dimensions are apt to be different. However, once more the problem of equipment supply is present. Sporting goods stores now stock tennis racquets and racquetball racquets, but the heavy wooden racquets used in paddle tennis are not usually seen, at least in the San Francisco Bay Area.

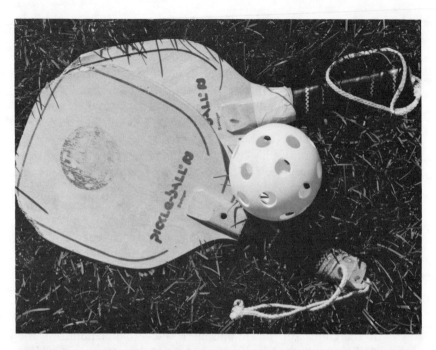

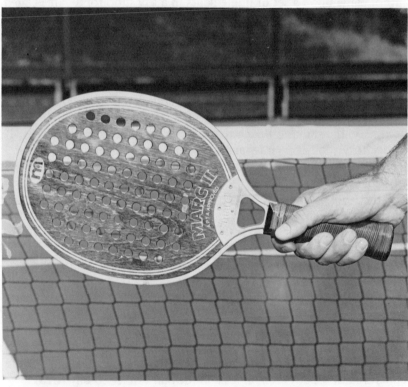

The game of paddle tennis is similar to platform tennis (Chapter 3) but there are a few real differences. The paddle tennis game does not allow play of the ball from the screens or fences. The paddle tennis net is stretched taut, at three feet, whereas the platform tennis net dips from 42 inches at the posts to 36 inches at the center. The platform tennis ball is a regulation tennis ball which has been punctured in order to deaden its bounce; platform tennis balls are softer and are manufactured especially for the game. Scoring for paddle tennis is the same as in platform tennis or (modern) tennis.

Court dimensions for paddle tennis are 50 by 20 feet with four service courts marked at 22 by 12 feet. West Coast courts also have restraint lines 12 feet from the net, parallel to the baselines, marking an area called the bucket.

The serve is underhand and may be taken out of hand or after one bounce. However, the server must stick to one or the other serve throughout a game after choosing which one to use. The server stands behind the baseline and serves to the court diagonally opposite.

In the singles game a one-bounce rule has been introduced in order to keep the server from rushing the net immediately after serving. The rule states that each player must allow the ball to bounce once before being permitted to volley.

On the West Coast the bucket area is used in doubles play. It is out of bounds for the players until the receiver has made the first strike on returning the ball.

Paddle tennis still has serious players of the game on the East Coast and in the Los Angeles area. An annual tournament is held, and play is fast and skillful. But the game has never regained the popularity it had during the Depression years.

All in all, the nature of playground racquet games is informality. With just the sketchiest of rules the players can have a great deal of fun. Children in particular can look forward to sharpening their skills for the more sophisticated sports awaiting them

Opposite, top: Pickle-ball racquet and ball. Bottom: The paddle tennis paddle is often identical to that used in platform tennis.

Organizations

United States Paddle Tennis Association
  Murray Geller, President
  189 Seeley St
  Brooklyn NY 11218

American Paddle Tennis League
  259 McCarty Dr
  Beverly Hills CA 90212

Afterword: Sideline Chatter

The view from the sidelines gives both the athlete and the fan a chance to size up the status of any game and the opportunity to make guesses as to where the game is going. So it is that in the period between the inception of this book and its publication there have been some changes observable in the world of racquet sports.

Court tennis and racquets are still thriving at the Boston Tennis and Racquets Club where the photographs in this book were taken, but the club has a new professional now, Mike Riley. He dreams of building someday, somewhere, a new full-sized racquets court. Barry Toates, the former professional, is in Newport, R.I., at the National tennis Court.

Squash is enjoying a mild boom throughout the United States although it is still overshadowed by racquetball, sometimes called the poor person's squash — now an undeserved epithet.

Platform tennis is still thriving on the East Coast, but the ambitious project at the College of Notre Dame in Belmont, Calif., where this book's pictures were taken, fell on hard times when the original promoters left the area. The courts are now in disrepair; the clubhouse has been vandalized. The college's new athletic director has hopes of reviving the sport. The San Francisco company for developing platform tennis is no longer in existence.

Table tennis and badminton have remained much the same in their development. Handball has been helped by the rush to build racquetball facilities.

Racquetball is still booming although there is a definite slowdown in sight. Early on the entrepreneurs of racquetball sports

165

complexes discovered that more than just racquetball courts had to be available in order to make a success of the sport facilities. New racquetball buildings include saunas, steam rooms, whirlpools, gymnasium facilities, child care centers, exercise programs, special events, and a wide variety of activities in order to attract and keep paying members. Some of the more elaborate developments even have full-sized swimming pools. Others have outdoor picnic and recreational areas. Professional players go on tour and put on demonstrations throughout the country. It is still a healthy, robust sport, but it is hard to guess how far it will continue to develop and grow.

Modern tennis is the golden sport on any level of play. One of the advantages the game has over almost all of the other racquet sports is that it is chiefly an outdoor game, in spite of the many indoor tennis complexes in existence. As such it entails far less trouble in maintenance. And when the weather is good many racquet sports players feel it is a pity to miss it by playing an indoor sport — a topic for a great debate perhaps.

Professional tennis has a new form of team tennis. Once known as World Team Tennis before it disbanded it is now known as Professional Team Tennis and is under the management of the ubiquitous Larry King. Team tennis uses five one-set matches, thus accentuating the team concept. Matches are played in singles and doubles (both men and women) and in mixed doubles. A special tie-breaker is used to determine a team winner when needed. At present there are eight teams in the league. King hopes for a 32 team league within the next six years, a hope which may or may not be overly optimistic.

Also, in the old but new world of tennis, two new almost-records were made within a week during the summer of 1982. Jimmy Connors needed four and a quarter hours to defeat John McEnroe in the Wimbledon finals, this even though two of the five sets played were shortened by tie breakers. Then, just a week later, McEnroe defeated Anders Jarryd in a Davis Cup singles match which took six hours and 32 minutes. This match allowed no tie-breakers, and included one set that went to the score of 15–17. As a sideliner it is tempting to have an opinion on the influence of tie-breakers in such high powered tennis.

Finally, back to court tennis again, the game to which is owed a debt of thanks for being the antecedent for racquet games. It was stated in Chapter 1 that just about the only place an interested spectator could catch a glimpse of the game was in a short segment of an old movie. There is a place where spectators are welcome to view the game: the Royal Tennis Court at Hampton Court Palace, London.

The official brochure (a handsome souvenir booklet) states, "The court is the oldest tennis court in use in the world; and the only one in Great Britain which the public are admitted (April–October) to see and, if play is in progress, to watch tennis being played."

In the booklet, the reader will find a diagram of the court, information as to the historical background of the Royal Tennis Court, a brief history of the game and a good discussion of the rules. But in a visit to the court itself, almost any racquet sports player should find an atavistic surge of recognition, as if coming home to basic origins — a feeling which cannot help improving participation in any racquet sport whether on the court or on the sidelines.

Bibliography

General

Morgenstern, Carol. *Playing the Racquets*. New York: Delta, 1980. Informal overview of modern tennis, squash, racquetball, paddle tennis, platform tennis and paddleball. Pictures and diagrams. Short chapter on history in general of racquetsports. Short chapter on warmups. Appendix of rules. No glossary. No index. (259 pages.)

Court Tennis

Arlott, John (editor). *The Oxford Companion to World Sports and Games*. London: Oxford University Press, 1975. Pages 821–832. Comprehensive history, including modern champions and courts still in use. Descriptions of how the games are played. Diagrams and illustrations.

The Royal Tennis Court, Hampton Court Palace. Published by the Committee of the Royal Tennis Court, Hampton Court Palace, London. Well Hall Press, Bromley, Kent, England. A handsome booklet, designed to give the newcomer a grasp of the sport. Diagrams, drawings, calligraphy, quotations from ancient manuscripts. (12 pages.)

Tennis

Clerici, Gianni. *The Ultimate Tennis Book*. Chicago: Follett, 1975. Lavishly produced. Elaborately illustrated. Good source of history of the game.

Collins, Bud, and Hollander, Sander. *Modern Encyclopedia of Tennis*. New York: Doubleday, 1980. Comprehensive. Authoritative. Interesting chapters on the 25 greatest players 1914 to 1945 and 1946 to 1979. Good treatment of the development of professional play and open competition. Hall of fame. Rules. Tennis records. Illustrated with photographs. (389 pages.)

Duggan, Moira. *The Tennis Catalogue*. New York: Macmillan, 1978. (Eugene Scott, editorial consultant.) Elaborate compilation of tennis equipment, facilities, published materials, paraphernalia, and many other items. Sections on careers, vacation and resort clinics, schools and camps. Glossary. Official rules. Index of manufacturers. Fully illustrated (photographs). However, much of the material is already dated.

Grimsley, Will. *Tennis; Its History, People and Events*. Englewood Cliffs, N.J.: Prentice-Hall, 1971. Easy to read. Filled with anecdotes. Particularly good in reference to men in the sport although includes a section for women. (379 pages.)

Harmon, Bob, with Montroe, Keith. *Use Your Head in Tennis*, revised edition. New York: Crowell, 1974. Psychology of winning tennis. Good section on "anticipation." Some drawings. (230 pages.)

Hovis, Ford (editor). *Tennis for Women*. New York: Doubleday, 1973. Ten chapters on various aspects of the game, each written by a woman professional. Clearly structured. Excellent illustrations (photographs). An outstanding book. (256 pages.)

King, Billie Jean. *Tennis to Win*. New York: Harper & Row, 1970. One of the best books in print on tennis basics. Drawings and diagrams. (157 pages.)

Koster, Rich. *The Tennis Bubble*. New York: Quadrangle/New York Times, 1976. Big money tennis, how it grew and where it is going. Problems, successes, failures. Of interest to the would-be professional or the student of the professional game. Some photographs. (209 pages.)

Leighton, Jim. *Inside Tennis: The Techniques of Winning*. Englewood Cliffs, N.J.: Prentice-Hall, 1969. Practical advice on strategy. Review of basics.

McPhee, John. *Levels of the Game*. New York: Farrar, Straus & Giroux, 1969. Written in *New Yorker* style about Arthur Ashe and Clark Graebner. Not easy reading but interesting. (150 pages.)

Medlycott, James. *100 Years of the Wimbledon Tennis Championships*. New York: Crescent Books, 1977. (Foreword by Don Budge.) Matches from 1877 through 1976. Lavishly illustrated with spectacular action shots. Eleven pages of Wimbledon results, including longest matches in each category. Sections on championship personalities, great games and fashions. (193 pages.)

Metzler, Paul. *Advanced Tennis*, revised edition. New York: Sterling,

1976. Good follow-up to his introductory book to tennis. Photographs and drawings.

————. *Getting Started in Tennis*. New York: Sterling, 1972. Simple, straightforward, good basic guide. No photographs. Good drawings. (128 pages.)

————. *Tennis Styles and Stylists*. New York: Macmillan, 1964. Interesting book of worldwide scope, featuring historic styles of play. Illustrated with pictures of tennis greats in action but slanted toward the men's game (11 women vs. 150 men). (217 pages.)

Ramo, Simon. *Extraordinary Tennis for the Ordinary Player*. New York: Crown, 1970. Nice little book for the club player. Practical. No photographs. Line drawings and diagrams. (158 pages.)

Riggs, Bobby, with McGann, George. *Court Hustler*. New York: J.B. Lippincott, 1973. Autobiography of an early tennis professional, a flamboyant cage rattler and flouter of convention. Written with verve, humor and spice. Concludes with a 16 page appendix called "Air Tight Tennis" filled with good, practical advice. (203 pages.)

Shannon, Bill (editor). *United States Tennis Association Official Encyclopedia of Tennis*, revised and updated edition. New York: Harper & Row, 1979. Fascinating reference book for the tennis buff. Filled with information including statistics and trivia. Profusely illustrated with photographs. Index. Glossary. (497 pages.)

Targhis, Barry. *Tennis and the Mind*. New York: Atheneum/SMI, 1977. (A *Tennis Magazine* book.) Written by a freelance who has five other tennis books to his credit. Interviews with tennis greats, including Evert, Borg, Laver, Riggs, Ashe, Connors, King, and many others. Short essays on mind-set and the game of tennis. (181 pages.)

Tennis Magazine, editors of. *Tennis Strokes and Strategies*. New York: Simon & Schuster, 1972. Good for basics. Well illustrated.

Tilden, Bill. *Match Play and the Spin of the Ball* (first published in 1925). Port Washington, N.Y.: Kennikat, 1969. A classic. Excellent analysis of footwork, grip, stroke and the function of spin. Must reading for the serious student of tennis. (177 pages.)

Wind, Herbert Warren. *Game, Set and Match*. New York: E.P. Dutton, 1979. Reprints 20 revised *New Yorker* articles. A history of the tennis boom of the 1960's and 70's. Good introduction featuring development of the game from 1881 to 1978. Informative reading about key tennis figures and events. (229 pages.)

Platform Tennis

Squires, Dick. *The Complete Book of Platform Tennis.* Boston: Houghton-Mifflin, 1974. Probably the best book for the beginner. Clear, concise, easy to understand. Illustrated.

Sullivan, George. *Paddle; The Beginners Guide to Platform Tennis.* New York: Coward, McCann & Geoghagan, 1976. Easy to read. Many photographs and diagrams. Authoritative. Glossary and index. (223 pages.)

Table Tennis

Miles, Dick. *The Game of Table Tennis.* Philadelphia: Lippincott, 1965. An older book than the one Miles did for *Sports Illustrated* but a good companion book. Illustrated by drawings. Rules. (141 pages.)

_____. *Sports Illustrated Table Tennis.* Philadelphia: Lippincott, 1975. A beginner's book. Illustrated by photographs. Rules. (95 pages.)

Phillip, David. *Table Tennis.* New York: Atheneum, 1975. Comprehensive treatment of the sport. Photographs, illustrations, and drawings. Good analysis of strokes. Glossary and rules. Advanced strategy. (213 pages.)

Purves, Jan. *Table Tennis.* San Diego: A.S. Barnes, 1942. Interesting if somewhat outdated. Written before the development of the sponge rubber paddle. For beginners. Illustrated.

Reisman, Marty. *The Money Player.* Merrick, N.Y., 1976. Story of professional table tennis.

Racquets

Arlott, John (editor). *The Oxford Companion to World Sports and Games.* London: Oxford University Press, 1975. Pages 813–818. Comprehensive history including champions and courts in use. Description of how game is played. Diagrams and illustrations.

Squash Racquets

Malloy, Al, with Lardner, Rex. *Sports Illustrated Book of Squash.* Philadelphia: Lippincott, 1963. Good introduction to the game. Drawings and diagrams. Basic shots. Glossary. (90 pages.)

Wood, Peter. *The Book of Squash.* Boston: Little, Brown, 1972. Excellent and detailed analysis of techniques. Game strategy. Illustrated. Photographs and diagrams.

Racquetball

Garfinkel, Charles. *Racquetball the Easy Way.* New York: Atheneum, 1978. Fully illustrated, including diagrams of shots. Interesting account of the Z serve introduced in play by Garfinkel during the April 1971 National Championships. Attention to game strategy and basics. Rules. Tournament information. (148 pages.)

Keele, Steve. *The Complete Book of Racquetball.* Chicago: DBI Books, 1976. Techniques up through advanced play. Illustrated. Diagrams and photographs.

Levy, Chuck. *Inside Racquetball.* Chicago: Regnery, 1973. The original racquetball book, still a classic. Fundamentals clearly described. Illustrated by photograph and diagram. Glossary. Index. (87 pages.)

Sauser, Jean, and Shay, Arthur. *Inside Racquetball for Women.* Chicago: Regnery, 1977. Fine introductory book for men or women. Illustrated. Diagrams and photographs.

Spear, Victor J. *How to Win at Racquetball.* Rockford, Ill., 1976. Game strategy for intermediate and advanced players.

_____. *Sports Illustrated Racquetball.* Philadelphia: Lippincott, 1979. Enthusiastic writer. Interesting and accurate history of the sport. Recent champions. Detailed analysis of strokes including photographs and diagrams. Chapter on conditioning. Glossary. (173 pages.)

Badminton

Devlin, Frank, with Lander, Rex. *Sports Illustrated Book of Badminton.* New York: Time-Life, 1967. For beginners and intermediate players. Official rules. Index. Fine illustrations and drawings. Glossary. (96 pages.)

Pelton, Barry C. *Badminton.* Englewod Cliffs, N.J.: Prentice-Hall, 1971. A primer for badminton beginners and teachers of the sport. Clearly written. Illustrated with drawings and diagrams. Index. Extensive annotated bibliography, including magazine articles and distributors of visual aids. (82 pages.)

Handball

McFarland, Wayne, and Smith, Philip. *Sports Illustrated Handball.* Philadelphia: Lippincott, 1976. Good basic book, clearly illustrated with drawings and diagrams. Some strategy. Glossary. (96 pages.)

O'Connell, Charlie. *Handball Illustrated.* New York: Ronald Press,

1968. A beginner's guide. Introductory techniques. Basic game. Rules. Glossary. Photographs and diagrams. (86 pages.)

Zafferano, George J. *Handball Basics.* New York: Stirling, 1977. Basic to intermediate and advanced. Analysis of responses to opponent's moves. Photographs and drawings. Rules. Glossary. Index. (192 pages.)

Index

A

ace 1
advantage 17, 20, 39, 57
Adidas 27, 29
Africa 2
Aiken 7
Aldilda 27
All-England Championship 125, 130
Amateur Athletic Union 146
American Badminton Association 125
American Paddle Tennis Association 45
American Paddle Tennis League 164
American Ping-Pong Association 62
American Platform Tennis Association
    45, 48, 59
American Professional Platform Tennis
    Association 58, 59
American Table Tennis Association 62
anthropology 1, 2, 144
approach volley 54
Arabia 78, 94
archeology 22
Association of Intercollegiate Athletics
    for Women 41
Asia 124
Australia 7, 94, 97
Auxere 2

B

backstop, Evans 46
badminton 22, 23, 159; clear 127, 132,
    133, 137; clothing 130; court 125;
    courtesies 142; drive 127, 132, 133,
    137; drop 133, 141; footwork 141;
    forehand 133, 135; the game 125–127;
    hand-in 130, 142; hand-out 130; his-
    tory 122–125; overhead 137; play 130;
    racquet 127; round-the-head 137, 141;
    rules (laws) 142; serve, short 130, 132;
    serve, long 130, 132, 135; shuttlecock
    125, 126, 127, 129; smash 127, 133
Badminton Association 125
Baggs, Mehan 145
Ball, Bat, and Bishop 1, 78
Bancroft 12, 27, 28
Barr 51
Barthelemey, A.D. 1
bat 11, 18, 66, 80
Bata Polymatch 29
battledore-and-shuttlecock 122–124
Beal, Frank P. 43
Beaufort, Duke of 122
Beginning Paddleball 108
Belmont 165
Berlin 124

175